MW00572197

Praise for *Cultural Meltdown*

"As a sociologist, Bill Donohue understands what happens to a society when the 'sacred canopy' of religion is ripped away. He knows that secularism is the 'heart of our moral crisis' and the cause of the cultural corruption we are experiencing. His inspiring book offers a way to extricate ourselves and our communities from the nihilism of a society without God and helps us find a way to achieve more meaning and purpose in our lives by recovering the timeless truths."

—*Anne Hendershott, Ph.D.*, Professor of Sociology
and Director of the Veritas Center for Ethics in Public
Life, Franciscan University of Steubenville, Ohio

"Donohue's response to our advanced cultural meltdown is not pessimism but pugnacity, in a full-throated defense of the Catholic vision of moral law as the basis of a good (though not perfect) moral order. Against the chaos and division of secular ideals 'we must reinvigorate and restore our Judeo-Christian heritage and focus on the hard work of achieving what is possible in the world.' People of faith have allowed the empty secular vision to prevail, but when they push back, things will change. In the end, the empty pretensions of secular elites will not be able to withstand the strong truths of the Christian faith, stubbornly maintained and defended by the Catholic Church."

—*Fr. Paul Sullins, Ph.D.*, Senior Research
Associate at the Ruth Institute

"In this much-needed book, Bill Donohue warns that a secular version of morality is destroying the seedbeds of civic virtues on which our American experiment depends. Fine social scientist that he is, Donohue documents the downward spiral in alarming detail. And as a happy warrior for religious and civil rights, he calls Catholics, evangelical Christians, Orthodox Jews, Mormons, and Muslims to stand up for their beliefs—for their own sakes and for the good of the country."

—*Mary Ann Glendon,* Professor of Law Emerita at Harvard
University and author of *In the Courts of Three Popes: An American
Lawyer and Diplomat in the West's Last Absolute Monarchy*

"Except that it's more enjoyable though every bit as tough, reading Bill Donohue's *Cultural Meltdown* is something like reading an Old Testament prophet. Like the prophets, Donohue skewers bad guys—doers of evil and sowers of confusion—with consistent vigor and style. Along the way, he also provides a helpful introduction to the history of ideas by documenting and analyzing the rise of overt, militant atheism in Western culture to its current position of cultural dominance. And, not least, he issues an invigorating call to Catholic laypeople to accept their responsibility for defending the Faith in an era of growing faithlessness. This is a must-read for serious Catholics."

—*Russell Shaw,* author, *American Church* and other works

"Societies, like the buildings we live and work in, usually do not just suddenly collapse. But they can be dismantled, brick by brick, by troubled people who, in pursuit of one secularist ideology or another, assert a moral imperative to become destroyers. Bill Donohue tells us who the thinkers and activists are who are trying to destroy our Judeo-Christian civilization. In doing so, he gives us valuable lessons on how to refute and resist the claims of those who feel no qualms about imposing their utopian nightmares on us all."

—*Fr. Gerald E. Murray,* Pastor, Church of the Holy Family, New York, and member of EWTN's *The Papal Posse*

Bill Donohue

CULTURAL MELTDOWN

The Secular Roots of
Our Moral Crisis

SOPHIA INSTITUTE PRESS
Manchester, New Hampshire

Sophia Institute Press
Box 5284, Manchester, NH 03108
1-800-888-9344
www.SophiaInstitute.com

Sophia Institute Press is a registered trademark of Sophia Institute.

hardcover ISBN 979-8-88911-246-4

ebook ISBN 979-8-88911-247-1

Library of Congress Control Number: 2024934425

First printing

For Walter Knysz Jr.

Contents

CULTURAL MELTDOWN

INTRODUCTION:
THE ORIGINS OF OUR MORAL CRISIS

WHAT MAKES INTELLECTUALS TICK?

NINETEENTH-CENTURY GERMAN PHILOSOPHER GEORG Wilhelm Friedrich Hegel lived in a time of great social upheaval. He referred to his era as *die verkehrte Welt*, or a "topsy-turvy world." We can identify with him. Our own society has gone topsy-turvy. What just yesterday was considered right is now deemed wrong — and vice versa. The question on everyone's mind is "What happened?"

In short, we are a country divided; our moral house is not in order, and the data prove it.

At the end of 2019, two-thirds of Americans said we are on the verge of a civil war.[1] In 2022, 79 percent of voters said the United States is "out of control." In 2018, almost half the

---

[1]   See the Georgetown Institute of Politics and Public Service Battleground Civility Poll, cited in Bill Donohue, "Will Our Culture War Become a Civil War?," Catholic

nation (49 percent) said moral values in the United States are "poor," which was the highest percentage ever recorded by Gallup since it first asked about this issue in 2002. By 2023, Gallup found that 54 percent of Americans said the state of moral values was "poor," and 33 percent rated them "only fair." A whopping 83 percent said they think moral values are getting worse.[2]

Alexis de Tocqueville, the great nineteenth-century Frenchman who visited our shores and wrote copiously about America, said that it is impossible to have a functioning society without a commonly held moral code. A century and a half later, the famous Russian freedom fighter, Aleksandr Solzhenitsyn, observed that no society could be free without an "objective legal scale."[3] He also said that the moral code was superior to the written law.

In this century, Rabbi Lord Jonathan Sacks argued that "to become moral, we have to make a commitment to some moral community and code," which for him meant adherence to our Judeo-Christian heritage.[4] He was not sanguine about the state of our moral house. Rather, Rabbi Sacks maintained that "our children and grandchildren are paying the price of abandoning a shared moral code: divided

League, November 1, 2019, https//www.catholicleague.org/will-our-culture-war-become-a-civil-war/.

[2] Megan Brenan, "Views of State of Moral Values in U.S. at New Low," Gallup, June 9, 2023, news.gallup.com/poll/506960/views-state-moral-values-new-low.aspx.

[3] Aleksandr I. Solzhenitsyn, *East and West* (New York: Harper and Row, 1980), 48.

[4] Jonathan Sacks, *Morality: Restoring the Common Good in Divided Times* (New York: Basic Books, 2020), 274.

societies, dysfunctional politics, high rates of drug abuse and suicide, increasingly unequal economies, a loss of respect for truth and the protocols of reasoning together, and the many other incivilities of contemporary life."[5]

Will Durant, the noted historian and philosopher, may not have personally believed in God, but he understood the importance of religion: "There is no significant example in history, before our time, of a society successfully maintaining moral life without the aid of religion."[6] He was seconded by the German Lutheran theologian Wolfhart Pannenberg, who wrote that "Western societies are well advised to recover their religious roots in a cultural tradition informed by Jewish and Christian beliefs."[7]

Easier said than done. The decline in religious beliefs and practices—what are called "measures of religiosity"—has been evident in virtually every Western nation for well over a half century.

We did not get to this point by accident. This book contends that our moral crisis is a reflection of the conflict between two competing visions of morality: one religious, the other secular. The former is grounded in our Judeo-Christian tradition; the latter is derived from radical notions of liberty and equality.

The religious vision acknowledges belief in God, truth, human nature, the natural law, moral absolutes, and

[5]   Ibid., 16.
[6]   Ibid., 277.
[7]   Wolfhart Pannenberg, "Christianity and the West," *First Things*, December 1994, https://www.firstthings.com/article/1994/12/christianity-and-the-west.

Original Sin. It recognizes the limitations of the human condition; and while it believes in progress, it manifestly rejects the idea of human perfectibility.

The secular vision promotes exactly the opposite view: God does not exist; truth is a mirage; human nature can be changed; there is no such thing as the natural law; there are no moral absolutes; and the idea of Original Sin is fanciful. Furthermore, as the secular vision considers the human condition to be infinitely malleable, it champions the idea of the perfectibility of man.

These two visions are fundamentally incompatible. As a society, and as individuals, we must choose one or the other. Either we believe in God's design, or we don't. It's that simple.

Dennis Prager succinctly describes certain hallmarks of the Torah rooted in some very basic categorical distinctions (distinctions, it is worth noting, that practicing Christians also accept).[8] For example, he notes distinctions between

✠ God and man,

✠ God and nature,

✠ man and animal,

✠ good and evil,

✠ life and death,

8   Dennis Prager, "Why Does the Bible Say 'Neither Sex May Wear the Clothing of the Other Sex'?," *Townhall*, October 12, 2022, townhall.com/columnists/dennisprager/2022/10/11/why-does-the-bible-say-neither-sex-may-wear-the-clothing-of-the-other-sex-n2614318.

✠ parent and child,

✠ holy and profane,

✠ male and female.

Those who adhere to the secular vision bristle at these binary differences. Their conception of man and society is enormously fluid. They conceive of the world as simply a social construct. Accordingly, there are no constants; everything can — and should — be reconstructed. Zeno, the first Stoic, wrote that men should live a life according to nature. Secularists reject this classical idea as fundamentally wrongheaded.

The Roman emperor Marcus Aurelius wrote, "The object of life is not to be on the side of the majority, but to escape finding oneself in the ranks of the insane."[9] The ranks of the insane seem, unfortunately, to be growing at an alarming rate — and much of the insanity can be found among some highly educated persons. Worse, highly educated intellectuals form others and shape our culture in ways that most Americans fail to appreciate. Of course, good ideas make for progress, enriching and enhancing human life in previously unimaginable ways. But bad ideas yield an altogether different fruit. And diabolical ideas produce unthinkable despair. We are living in a time when some very bad ideas about the world have gained astonishing acquiescence, producing tremendous social turmoil.

[9]   H. W. Crocker III, "Post-Sanity America," *Crisis Magazine*, October 12, 2022, https://www.crisismagazine.com/2022/post-sanity-america.

As a professor and as an activist, I have worked for decades with learned men and women who are specialists in their fields. Many are good people, doing their best to advance knowledge and serve society. But many others are strange and dysfunctional—and indeed, some seem profoundly unhappy. Alienated from society, they are often resentful and angry. And most of them are left-wing. (Unless otherwise noted, when I refer to intellectuals, I will mean left-wing intellectuals.)

What makes these intellectuals tick? A number of things. They have a passionate yearning for equality, in all of its manifestations, of all types; they see oppression everywhere; they rail against any restrictions on sexuality; they subscribe to moral relativism; they have a desperate need for meaning and purpose; they deny the existence of human nature; and they reject God.

If their secular vision were merely an expression of their own personal beliefs, it would not matter much. But their radical ideas about liberty and equality do not linger in the classroom; they lunge out into the rest of society and threaten all of us. From the academy, left-wing ideology first colonized the arts, the entertainment industry, the media, the publishing houses, the large-scale foundations, and the nonprofit advocacy organizations. Now it is prevalent in big corporations, the medical profession, and even the military, at least in the higher echelons of these places. From efforts to teach white students that they are inherently racist to encouraging young kids to question whether they are really boys or girls, left-wing ideas have aggressively advanced throughout our civilization. This explains the insanity of our time: madness has been mainstreamed.

The widespread adoption of the secular vision has not only resulted in a cultural meltdown—it has also clashed with our Judeo-Christian heritage. Surveys and election data show that roughly half the nation still maintains an allegiance to our religious roots; the other half has become thoroughly secularized. This situation is precariously unstable. At some point, one viewpoint will likely eclipse the other. But while the ruling class has two feet in the secular camp, there is one institution that stands in the way of a secular triumph: the Catholic Church.

The Catholic Church teaches that all human beings are made in the image and likeness of God. She proclaims that all men and all women possess equal dignity, ordained by God. We are all expected to conform our behavior to the tenets of the natural law, and we all intuitively know the difference between right and wrong, good and evil. Even the Greeks and Romans understood the ability of reason to recognize virtue; but it was Thomas Aquinas, standing on the shoulders of Aristotle and Cicero, who showed that the natural law must be subordinate to—though never in conflict with—the divine law. Though we are inherently flawed, we are capable of knowing the truth because we have the capacity to reason.

However, what was accepted wisdom in the Middle Ages came under attack during the seventeenth- and eighteenth-century Enlightenment. The belief in reason, and in progress, certainly produced great advances in science and technology. But putting everything under the microscope of rationalism obscured many nonrational, nonscientific truths that had long animated the human soul, such as the nature of goodness, the value of custom, the wisdom of tradition, the importance of beauty—indeed, the purpose of life itself.

But the thinkers of the Enlightenment had a contempt for the past that engendered a particular contempt for Christianity. Voltaire, a major figure in the French Enlightenment, hated the Church. He argued that "every man of sense, every good man ought to hold the Christian sect in horror."[10] He believed in freedom of speech and tolerance for everyone—except Catholics. Denis Diderot, another influential Enlightenment figure, said the Christian religion "is the most absurd and atrocious in its dogmas," and he blamed it for disturbing "public tranquility."[11] Jean-Jacques Rousseau outdid them all: his radical egalitarian views made him the intellectual father to Robespierre and his Reign of Terror, during which Catholic nuns and priests were raped and murdered by the thousands, and churches were burnt to the ground—all in the name of "enlightened" thought.

The tradition of bashing the Catholic Church was carried on after the Enlightenment by Marx and Engels. But it was another German writer, Friedrich Nietzsche, who

---

[10] Alberto M. Piedra, "Enlightenment, Age of the," in *Encyclopedia of Catholic Social Thought, Social Science, and Social Policy*, ed. Michael L. Coulter, Stephen M. Krason, Richard S. Myers, and Joseph A. Varacalli (Lanham, MD: Scarecrow Press, 2007), 360.

[11] Ibid.

declared in 1882 that "God is dead." According to many historians, this was a turning point in intellectual history: legions of artists and writers began to express their disdain for Christianity, and for the virtues that it sustains. Permissive notions about sexuality, which devalue marriage and the family, became ubiquitous. Sexual satisfaction was said to rest with the emancipation of the "pleasure principle," or the satisfaction of the id — and no amount of sexually transmitted disease, or increasingly reported unhappiness, seemed to challenge their perverted idea of sexual liberation. Indeed, their belief that there is no truth now allows today's intellectuals to think that even the sexes are meaningless and interchangeable.

We are told that if we just listen to the intellectuals, we will be able to establish a perfect society, where oppression is nonexistent and sexual freedom will abound. (Notice that sexual freedom and societal freedom are always intertwined.) But such promises have been the snake oil of radicals since time immemorial.

Intellectuals are always seeking to liberate us from something — if only we give them the power they crave. Certainly they want power. If only they understood the limitations of the human condition, they might not be so angry with the status quo, so desperate to change it. But they are. Indeed, they are angry that more Americans are not as angry about everything that angers them!

But our moral crisis will not abate until we are once again able to achieve a religious moral consensus. The secular conception of man and society is not only not possible, but attempts to actualize it have inevitably led to chaos and division. We must reinvigorate and restore our Judeo-Christian heritage and focus on the hard work of achieving what is possible in the world rather than chasing the empty dreams of the secularists.

PART I

CULTURE SHOCK

CHAPTER 1

CLASH OF CULTURES

THE RELIGIOUS-SECULAR DIVIDE

INTELLECTUALS TEND TO REGARD themselves highly—even when others do not. When they feel underappreciated, they console themselves by looking down on the plebeians. They assure themselves that we are too parochial and ignorant to recognize their superiority. If only we were more sophisticated, we wouldn't look to God for answers to personal and social problems. We would look to them. Yes, they often sneer—they love to sneer—at God and His faithful.

Since the founding of America, there has always been religious tension in the country. For generations, a WASP elite practiced anti-Catholicism, and many Protestant sects challenged each other's conceptions of truth. But then things changed: in the late 1960s, a new secular elite, led by leftist intellectuals, became the biggest bigots on the block. They took aim at Catholics, at evangelical Christians, indeed at everyone who subscribed to traditional moral values (they didn't bother with mainline Protestant denominations; they had become too secularized to matter).

Since the 1960s, the federal government, now grown to gargantuan proportions, has also become an enormous force for religious bigotry. To be sure, most of those who serve in federal, state, and local government agencies are good men and women. But there are also platoons of government foot soldiers who have besieged religion, especially Christianity.[12] Here is just a sampling of recent examples.

When COVID hit, secular-minded mayors in one city after another put restrictions on houses of worship, restrictions far more severe than those put on department stores and other businesses. One liberal blogger, Nate Silver, saw the irony. "It's kind of crazy (and tells you a lot about who was writing the restrictions) that churches in some jurisdictions were subject to more restrictions than museums."[13] When San Francisco archbishop Salvatore Cordileone protested, saying churches were being discriminated against, government officials refused to even reply.[14]

[12] The beliefs of Orthodox Jews, Mormons, and Muslims are not well received by the secular elite, but they are too small to worry about, at least for now. Hence, the focus on Catholics and evangelical Christians.

[13] Glenn H. Reynolds, "The COVID Lockdown Scolds Killed People—but They Still Have No Shame," *New York Post*, April 24, 2023, nypost.com/2023/04/24/the-covid-lockdown-scolds-killed-people-but-they-still-have-no-shame.

[14] Archbishop Cordileone made his comment in an interview with Raymond Arroyo on the EWTN show *The World Over*, June 1, 2023.

Also, during the pandemic shutdowns, secular elites in government allowed throngs of young people to ignore social distancing norms and conferred their blessing on "social justice" demonstrations. The mayor of New York City, Bill de Blasio, was asked how he could justify an exception to his ironclad prohibitions when even churchgoers were barred from attending services. "Four hundred years of American racism, I'm sorry, that is not the same question as the understandably aggrieved store owner or devout religious person who wants to go back to services."[15] His purported interest in public health took a back seat to his political agenda.

He would never have allowed throngs of pro-life demonstrators to ignore his "social distancing" dictum, despite the tens of millions of unborn corpses, because he is on the opposite side of that fundamental issue of life and death. In fact, de Blasio even demonized efforts by Rev. Franklin Graham to bring seventy-two doctors, nurses, and other medical personnel from an evangelical group, Samaritan's Purse, to set up a sixty-eight-bed facility in Central Park because Graham believes in marriage between a man and a woman.

Though there is no evidence that the minister had ever turned down services of any kind to anyone, de Blasio said he was worried that he might discriminate against gays. In fact, like the militant secularist that he is, he sent "monitors" to find out if there was "going to be an approach that was truly consistent with the values and laws of New York

---

[15] Bill Donohue, "De Blasio and Cuomo Get Creamed in Court," Catholic League, July 31, 2020, https://www.catholicleague. org/de-blasio-and-cuomo-get-creamed-in-court-2/.

City."[16] Instead of thanking Graham for bringing his volunteer medical staff to New York, de Blasio acted as though the reverend was embarking on some kind of Christian crusade, trying to bring a Christian "virus" to the Big Apple.

But New York is hardly alone. For twelve years, the city of Boston had authorized 284 flags to fly atop a city flagpole outside of city hall, representing a myriad of government and private interests. But in 2018 it turned down a request by Camp Constitution to fly what they described as a "Christian" flag, maintaining that to do so would amount to government endorsement of religion. But Gay Pride flags were allowed; only Christian flags were banned. The Christian group sued and the Supreme Court voted unanimously to allow the Christian flag. The high court ruled that the flagpole represented a public forum, and therefore the government could not discriminate on the basis of the religious viewpoint of Camp Constitution.[17] But even the Supreme Court is now under constant attack from leftists.

The legal resolution of this particular issue notwithstanding, why did secular elites in Boston decide to cherry-pick one group and deny it the right to fly their Christian flag when they had no problem honoring the flags

---

[16] Bill Donohue, "De Blasio Fears 'Christian Virus,'" Catholic League, April 3, 2020, http://www.catholicleague.org/de-blasio-fears-christian-virus/.

[17] Ariane de Vogue, Tierney Sneed, and Devan Cole, "Supreme Court Says Boston Violated First Amendment Rights of Group Seeking to Raise a Christian Flag outside City Hall," *CNN*, May 2, 2022, edition.cnn.com/2022/05/02/politics/boston-free-speech-flagpole-case-supreme-court/index.html.

of Communist nations? Why was rejecting the Christian flag so important to them that they appealed lower court rulings to the highest court in the land? Let's face it, they did so because of their deep-seated anti-Christian animus.

It's not just secular-run municipalities that harbor ill will toward Christians. Some in the federal government do as well. In early 2023, an FBI whistleblower revealed that the Richmond field office was investigating "Radical-Traditionalist Catholics," or what they called RTCs. When I first learned of this, I was dumbfounded. I come from an Irish Catholic family where many of the men served in law enforcement. The idea that the FBI would conduct a probe of Catholics who have no record of criminality was very upsetting. The agency said it distinguished between RTCs and "traditionalist" Catholics. I was skeptical. I was born Catholic; I wasn't born yesterday. I made a public statement, questioning, "What's next? Will it be a war on Catholics who are orthodox?"

As it turned out, I was right. In the spring of 2023, thanks to the leadership of Rep. Jim Jordan, chairman of the House Judiciary Committee, we learned that "mainline" Catholics and dioceses were being monitored. The FBI sought to get loyal sons and daughters of the Catholic Church to spy on each other. During the summer, it was revealed that it was not just the Richmond branch of the FBI that was involved: the Los Angeles, Milwaukee, and Portland field offices also participated in this plan. This prompted me to ask Rep. Jordan to ask FBI Director Christopher Wray a series of questions. Here are some of them:

✠ "On what basis did the FBI conclude that these [RTC] Catholics warranted a probe? Do they have a history of violence? If so, where is the evidence? If not, why were they singled out?"

✠ "On what basis did the FBI decide it was necessary to enlist 'mainline Catholics' to spy on their fellow parishioners? Where is the evidence that ordinary practicing Catholics pose a security threat to the United States or to other law-abiding Americans?"[18]

Later in the year, Attorney General Merrick Garland testified before Jordan's panel. Like Wray, who claimed he was "aghast" at the news of the FBI operation, Garland said that he, too, knew nothing about it and that he was "appalled" by the accounts. I asked in writing, and on TV, why no one has been held accountable. I also asked if the probe of Catholics initiated from outside the FBI; I wouldn't be surprised if it did.[19]

At the end of 2023, the House Select Subcommittee on the Weaponization of the FBI issued a report on the Bureau's investigation of Catholics. I contacted Jordan again (the subcommittee is under his tutelage) about new developments.

---

[18] "FBI War on Catholics Heats Up; So Does Our Response," Catholic League, September 20, 2023, http://www.catholicleague.org/fbi-war-on-catholics-heats-up-so-does-our-response/.

[19] I appeared on *The World Over*, EWTN, September 28, 2023. See also Bill Donohue, "Garland Goes Mute about FBI Catholic Probe," Catholic League, September 21, 2023, https://www.catholicleague.org/garland-goes-mute-about-fbi-catholic-probe/.

It was revealed that the FBI relied on profoundly left-wing journalistic sources and organizations for information about the Catholic Church, the most notorious of which was the Southern Poverty Law Center. Worse, the goal of the Catholic probe was to share the information obtained by the Richmond field office with offices across the country. In other words, this may have begun as a regional issue, but the plan was to disseminate the information nationwide. It was painfully obvious that an anti-Catholic entity was operating within the FBI.

In my December 6, 2023 letter to Jordan, I asked him to address these issues, and to inquire why no FBI employee was disciplined. I also asked him to find out how this all started and whether outsiders were involved in the crafting of this caper.[20]

Jordan's staff was appreciative of our efforts and interest in this matter. But it is a disturbing sign that the radical, secular, aggressive, anti-American, and anti-religious mindset has infiltrated the highest ranks of the FBI.

PROFILE OF SECULARISTS

Who are the people most likely to be secularists? As virtually every survey reveals, young people, liberals, and Democrats are by far the most secular segment of the population. Furthermore, a Gallup poll done in 2022 found that "belief in God has fallen the most in recent years among young adults

---

[20] "Rep. Jordan Asked to Continue to Pursue FBI," Catholic League, December 6, 2023, https://www.catholicleague.org/rep-jordan-asked-to-continue-to-pursue-fbi/.

and people on the left of the political spectrum (liberals and Democrats). These groups show drops of 10 or more percentage points comparing the 2022 figures to an average of the 2013–2017 polls."[21]

We also know that in 2021, 45 percent of Democrats said they were agnostic, atheist, or had no religious affiliation. For Republicans, the figure was only 19 percent.[22] Democrats have become so secular that Gallup found the percentage who identify as religious dropped from 60 percent in 1999 to 37 percent in 2023.[23]

The impact that young people, liberals, and Democrats have on "measures of religiosity" is considerable. Gallup reported in 2022 that belief in God had dipped to 81 percent, a new low. In the 1940s, 1950s, and 1960s, "a consistent 98% said they believed in God."[24]

[21] Jeffrey M. Jones, "Belief in God in U.S. Dips to 81%, a New Low," Gallup, June 17, 2022, news.gallup.com/poll/393737/belief-god-dips-new-low.aspx.

[22] "Why Democrats Are Less Religious than Republicans," Religion Unplugged, January 31, 2023, religionunplugged.com/news/2023/1/23/analysis-data-shows-democrats-increasingly-becoming-the-party-of-non-religious-voters.

[23] Jeffrey M. Jones, "In U.S., 47% Identify as Religious, 33% as Spiritual," Gallup, September 22, 2023, https://news.gallup.com/poll/511133/identify-religious-spiritual.aspx. It is for this reason that when comparing religious Americans to secular Americans, if religious affiliation is not identified in a survey, being a liberal or a Democrat will be treated as representative of secular thought; similarly, those who identify as a conservative or a Republican will be treated as representative of the religious vision.

[24] Jones, "Belief in God."

Education level is also a revealing indicator of secularism. Poll after poll shows that college graduates are more secular than those who have not achieved a degree; those with post-graduate degrees are even more secular.[25] In other words, the intellectuals who work in higher education do a masterful job at secularizing their students.

They have also succeeded in fomenting a great deal of secularist animosity toward religion and religious people. A 2020 Cato survey found that 77 percent of conservatives, 64 percent of moderates, and 52 percent of liberals said they were afraid to say what they think. On the subject of religion, 33 percent of Democrats felt free to express their viewpoint in most situations on a daily basis, but the figure for Republicans was just 14 percent; it was 32 percent for liberals and 18 percent for conservatives.

In 2021, a Lifeway Research survey found that "nearly 60% agreed that 'Christians increasingly are confronted by intolerance in America today.'" Those who regularly attend religious services were even more likely to say this is true. As expected, the religiously unaffiliated were the least likely to agree.[26] In 2022, a McLaughlin survey commissioned by the Catholic League found that 62 percent of Catholics

25 Bill Donohue, "Revealing Data on Education and Religion," Catholic League, August 17, 2023, https://www.catholicleague. org/revealing-data-on-education-and-religion/.
26 "Most Americans Think Religious Freedom Is In Decline," *Christian Post*, July 15, 2022, https://www.christianpost.com/news/most-americans-believe-religious-freedom-is-in-decline-survey.html.

agreed that "it is getting harder to practice your faith publicly in America."[27]

In 2022, Supreme Court Justice Samuel Alito wrote the majority opinion overturning *Roe v. Wade*, which greatly upset militant secularists. In an address he made in Rome, he talked about a "growing hostility to religion, or at least the traditional religious beliefs that are contrary to the new moral code that is ascendant in some sectors."[28] He was unfairly accused of harboring a "deeper, darker message," one that suggests the only remedy to a secular society is "state-sponsored indoctrination," something he never said or implied.[29]

It's also getting harder for students who believe in traditional moral values to express themselves on college campuses. In 2023, the Foundation for Individual Rights and Expression (FIRE) released its annual survey on the status of free speech on campus. In a survey of almost forty-five thousand college students from 201 colleges, it found that liberals—who are disproportionately secularists—were the most intolerant of free speech.

---

[27] Bill Donohue, "Intolerance for Free Speech Is Spiking," Catholic League, November 10, 2022, www.catholicleague.org/intolerance-for-free-speech-is-spiking/.

[28] Greg Stohr, "Alito, Supreme Court's Abortion Opinion Author, Decries 'Hostility to Religion,'" Bloomberg, July 28, 2022, bloomberg.com/news/articles/2022-07-28/alito-abortion-opinion-author-decries-hostility-to-religion.

[29] Dahlia Lithwick and Mark Joseph Stern, "Alito's Speech Mocking Foreign Leaders Has a Deeper, Darker Message," *Slate*, July 29, 2022, https://slate.com/news-and-politics/2022/07/alito-rome-religious-liberty-foreign-leaders-secularism.html.

Real Clear Opinion Research has also researched free speech. According to its 2023 survey results on this topic, Democrats were the least supportive of free speech and the most supportive of censoring speech they found disagreeable. In fact, a third said Americans have "too much freedom." This was in stark contrast to 14.6 percent of Republicans.[30]

Naturally, liberals claim this is all nonsense. They insist that they believe in free speech, and they point to one of their own groups, the ACLU, as being one of the most well-known champions of free speech. Nevertheless, it is not conservatives who are shouting down liberals on campus. As for the ACLU, its reputation is largely overblown. In 1936, it threatened to sue the *American Mercury* simply because the magazine published an article that was critical of ... the ACLU. H. L. Mencken was asked *by both parties* to render an objective judgment about the article; he concluded there was nothing libelous about it.[31] And while the ACLU famously defends the free speech of neo-Nazis—who, while reprehensible, are today an insignificant political force—it is reliably missing in action when it comes to defending the free speech rights of pro-life activists, who represent a real political threat to the pro-abortion industry and the opinions of the ruling class.

I found out how insincere the ACLU is about free speech when I debated its president, Norman Dorsen, at

---

[30] Carl M. Cannon, "Poll: Is Censorship a Partisan Issue?," Real-ClearPolitics, September 22, 2023, https://www.realclearpolitics.com/real_clear_opinion_research/poll_is_censorship_a_partisan_issue_149790.html.

[31] William A. Donohue, *The Politics of the American Civil Liberties Union* (New Brunswick, NJ: Transaction Press, 1985), 229–238.

Harvard University in the early 1990s. Both the ACLU chapter, which sponsored Dorsen, and the Federalist Society chapter, which sponsored me, agreed to release a video of the debate once it was over. But after the (very long) debate, the ACLU chapter reneged on their agreement to release the video. The Harvard law faculty was asked to review the controversy and render a judgment. They cowardly decided that the video could be released provided both Dorsen and I agreed to do so, knowing full well that Dorsen would withhold consent. So much for cherishing free speech.

Matters have only gotten worse on college campuses. As the FIRE survey found, liberals were more likely to oppose those whom they considered to be controversial speakers, namely conservatives, and were more likely to say it was acceptable to shout them down. Almost half thought it was okay to block them from entering the campus. Astonishingly, a quarter (25 percent) approved of using violence to stop a campus speech. When we consider that, according to FIRE, 53 percent of college students describe themselves as "left of center" and only 20 percent identify as "right of center," it is quite clear who values free speech and who does not.

Religious students, who tend to be conservatives, reported the most reluctance to express themselves. Perhaps that is because two of the subjects that all students said were the most difficult to discuss on campus were abortion and transgender issues—and students who hold to Christian teachings on sexual ethics, for example, are often intimidated into keeping silent on these matters. Meanwhile, most professors and students can feel comfortable saying more or less whatever they want.[32]

A survey released by *Newsweek* around the same time revealed that 44 percent of those between the ages of twenty-five and forty-four want to make "misgendering"—using the "wrong" pronoun to describe a transgender person—a criminal offense. Among those between the ages of thirty-five and forty-four, 38 percent support treating this as a crime. The overall figure for Americans was 19 percent.[33]

Over the past few decades, many noted liberals have commented that they no longer feel comfortable associating with liberals. That's because so many liberals have moved left, and become more extreme. Old-time liberals such as Alan Dershowitz now look like they are conservatives. But he didn't really change. He may have defended Trump against impeachment charges, but he never voted for him. It was liberalism that changed. And that change is reflected in the Democratic Party.

When I was growing up in New York, practically all the Catholics I knew were Democrats. Protestants were for Republicans; Catholics and Jews were for Democrats. That changed dramatically in the late 1960s and the early 1970s when Catholics no longer felt wanted in the Democratic Party. Many felt politically homeless; more than a few became Republicans, or independents.

---

[32] Bill Donohue, "The Alarming Assault on Free Speech," Catholic League, August 1, 2023, https://www.catholicleague.org/the-alarming-assault-on-free-speech/.

[33] Ibid.

Today, Democrats do not look kindly on Catholics. A 2023 survey by the Pew Research Center disclosed that more Democrats had an unfavorable view of Catholics (25 percent) than had a favorable view of them (22 percent). Interestingly, Democrats look more favorably on Muslims and atheists.[34]

This is truly remarkable. It wasn't too long ago that Catholics were the mainstay of the Democratic Party. That Democrats find atheists more appealing than Catholics is not completely shocking, given how secular Democrats have become. But when Democrats look upon Muslims—who do have a religious faith—more favorably than Catholics, that says a great deal about the changing face of the party.

This shift was not lost on Tulsi Gabbard, the former Democrat congresswoman from Hawaii. After leaving office, she also left her party. In 2023, she said that "one of the main reasons why I chose to leave the Democratic Party [is] because I saw increasingly how not only were they trying to erase any mention of God, [but they were also] attacking people of faith, attacking people of spirituality, especially Christians."[35]

---

[34] Patricia Tevington, "Americans Feel More Positive than Negative about Jews, Mainline Protestants, Catholics," Pew Research Center, March 15, 2023, 19, https://www.pewresearch.org/religion/wp-content/uploads/sites/7/2023/03/PF_2023.03.15_religion-favorability_REPORT.pdf.

[35] Joshua Klein, "Tulsi Gabbard Says Attacks on Faith, God Drove Her to Leave Democrats: Many Think 'They Are God,'" Breitbart, March 20, 2023, breitbart.com/politics/2023/03/20/tulsi-gabbard-says-attacks-faith-god-drove-her-leave-democrats-many-think-they-are-god.

The attacks she references are real, and they have consequences. For example, religious Americans are more likely to be wary of expressing themselves in public. Why? Secularists who occupy a disproportionate share of elite positions in society exude intolerance for religion, which creates a "chilling effect" on the speech of religious Americans. (Ironically, it is the grand thinkers who applaud themselves on being the most tolerant of our citizens.) And this is no matter of mistaken perception. Here are a few concrete examples of why religious Americans are cautious about expressing themselves in public.

✠ In 2023, a dozen Catholic students and their chaperones from a Greenville, South Carolina, Catholic high school were ordered out of the Smithsonian National Air and Space Museum in Washington, D.C., because they wore beanies with pro-life messages. In town for the annual March for Life, they were mocked and cursed at by the museum staff.

✠ In 2023, Ivan Provorov, a hockey player for the Philadelphia Flyers, skipped the warm-ups on Pride Night because he was expected to wear a pro-Pride jersey. A member of the Russian Orthodox Church, he was subjected to hate speech by some fans and commentators. "I respect everybody's choices," he said. "My choice is to stay true to myself and my religion."

✠ In 2023, Paul Shoro, a black Christian, walked into the Mall of America in

Bloomington, Minnesota, wearing a T-shirt that read "Jesus is the only way." Security officers, responding to complaints, said to him, "If you want to shop here you need to take off that shirt." He was explicitly told that "Jesus is associated with religion and it is offending people."

✣ In 2022, three students at the University of Idaho were asked by a fellow student why the Christian Legal Society (to which they belonged) required its members to believe in the Christian understanding of marriage. After they gave a biblical answer, the university's Office of Civil Rights and Investigation censored their speech, ordering the Christian students not to communicate with the complaining student.

✣ In 2022, a Michigan junior high school student filed suit in U.S. District Court against his high school district because he was suspended for three days the previous fall for stating his Christian beliefs in a private text conversation in a school hallway.

✣ In 2022, a U.S. Army veteran was arrested for holding a sign that read "God bless the homeless vets." He was standing in front of city hall in Alpharetta, a town in Georgia. He was handcuffed by police and charged with "panhandling," though all he did was hold the sign. He sued a year later.

✠ In 2021, a scholar-in-residence at Christopher
Newport University in Newport News, Virginia, who "proudly and openly identified as
a Christian woman of color," was condemned
for criticizing DC Comics' decision to make
Superman's son bisexual. Students protested
and wanted her removed from the campus,
despite the fact that she deleted her tweet.[36]

These examples—and there are innumerable more like
them—would be less dramatic if there were equivalent examples of religious Americans silencing the speech of secular
Americans. But there are not. Almost always, it's people of
faith who are being censored.

The religious-secular divide is most evident with respect
to moral issues. In 2022, Gallup found a considerable gap
between self-described liberals and conservatives on a range
of moral issues, especially those concerning abortion, gay or
lesbian relations, teenage sex, and doctor-assisted suicide.
Liberals were much more likely than conservatives to approve of these behaviors. Other issues about which liberals
were more enthusiastic included premarital sex, stem cell
research, pornography, polygamy, and suicide.[37]

[36] Bill Donohue, "War on Religion Spiking in U.S. and U.K.,"
Catholic League, February 6, 2023, https://www.catholicleague.
org/war-on-religion-spiking-in-us-and-uk/.

[37] Megan Brenan, "Americas Say Birth Control, Divorce Most
'Morally Acceptable,'" Gallup, June 9, 2022, https://news.gal-
lup.com/poll/393515/americans-say-birth-control-divorce-
morally-acceptable.aspx.

It is not hard to figure out the reasons for these opposing moral views. The secular, or liberal, vision is much more individualistic than the religious, or conservative. Matters involving sexuality, in particular, are seen by liberals to be in the arena of self-expression. Conservatives are more likely to jealously guard the integrity of marriage and the family, and to condemn perceived threats to these keystone institutions. The liberal support for suicide is another expression of the valuing of individual autonomy over religious norms.

The underlying differences between these two strands of thought can be seen when we consider an issue that arose during the COVID pandemic. A Pew Research Center survey asked respondents what should happen if ventilators were in short supply. Whom should we serve first—those who are most in need at the moment, or those most likely to recover?

The answer, as with so many ethical issues, turns on religion. The majority of those who are religiously affiliated said that those who are most in need of a ventilator at the moment should take priority; the majority of the religiously unaffiliated (mostly agnostics and atheists) said those who are the most likely to recover should get it.[38]

Secularists, it is evident, have adopted a utilitarian ethic like that espoused by the British philosopher Jeremy Bentham. He maintained that morality was best served by striving for the greatest good for the greatest number of

[38] Bill Donohue, "Atheists Elicit an Amoral Ethics," Catholic League, April 30, 2020, https://www.catholicleague.org/atheists-elicit-an-amoral-ethics/.

people. Such a philosophy advantages the powerful and the healthy at the expense of the weak. Indeed, it can even be used to justify slavery and euthanasia. Amoral stances can yield immoral consequences.

It is hard to reconcile these visions of morality, which is why we are in a moral crisis. Among other problems with the secular perspective, at least in its more extreme manifestation, is its defiance of basic sociological insights about the social order. The proposition that every individual should be free to adopt his own moral code is sociologically inane. It is a prescription for moral anarchy. In the absence of a moral baseline that is generally acknowledged and accepted, society is bound to crumble.

No society can exist without a moral consensus. That consensus needn't be universal. But there must be a general agreement about fundamental things. Currently, our society is suffering because two competing understandings of morality are dueling for dominance. While there is no way to predict how long we can tolerate the conflict, until one side succeeds in becoming dominant, the tension in our land will only grow worse, for both sides. It's a lose-lose, high-stakes situation, and the impact on society is dramatic.

In 2022, for example, the Catholic League, using a study by the Pew Research Center, compared opinions in the twelve most religious states to those in the twelve least religious states on several issues. The twelve most religious states, as determined by the percent of adults who identify as highly religious, are, from top to bottom: Alabama, Mississippi, Tennessee, Louisiana, Arkansas, South Carolina, West

Virginia, Georgia, Oklahoma, North Carolina, Texas, and Utah. The twelve least religious states are, from top to bottom: New Hampshire, Massachusetts, Vermont, Maine, Connecticut, Wisconsin, Washington, Alaska, New York, Hawaii, Colorado, and Oregon.

In eight of the twelve most religious states, there were religious liberty laws in place; only one of the twelve least religious states had such a protective law. The average percentage of pregnancies aborted per one hundred thousand in the most religious states was 11.23 percent; in the least religious states it was 17.66 percent. All twelve of the most religious states have restrictive abortion laws; one in twelve of the least religious states has such a law. On the issue of school choice, eleven of twelve of the most religious states have some sort of program that allows for private school choice; three of twelve of the least religious states have such a program. When comparing rates of drug overdose and suicide, however, the differences were negligible.[39]

Lawmakers can do little to prevent self-destruction, but they can pass laws that affect religious liberty, abortion, and school choice, and on these issues, the most religious states do a much better job.

For obvious reasons, abortion is the most serious and contentious moral issue of our day. The overturning of *Roe v. Wade* was a significant legal change, but it did nothing to change the morality of abortion.

[39] Bill Donohue, "Comparing Religious States to Secular States," Catholic League, February 17, 2022, https://www.catholicleague.org/comparing-religious-states-to-secular-states/.

In 2022, a Rasmussen survey of American voters found that only 5 percent believe abortion should be legal in all cases, with no restrictions whatsoever.[40] In 2023, a Knights of Columbus–Marist poll found that while six in ten adults call themselves "pro-choice," seven in ten of them believe there should be restrictions on abortion. It also found that nine in ten adults support crisis pregnancy centers.[41]

In 2022, the Pew Research Center released the most comprehensive survey on abortion it ever took. It found that only one in five say abortion should be legal in all cases. It also found that those on both sides of this issue are okay with making some exceptions to their position.[42]

In other words, while Americans want abortion to be legal in some cases, they are not in favor of abortion on demand, which is what *Roe* effectively enforced. This has consistently been the case for decades.

The Pew survey is helpful because it examined the religious-secular divide on abortion. It found that religion shapes a person's views about abortion in a fundamental way. For

[40] Bill Donohue, "5% of Voters Support No Limits on Abortion," Catholic League, June 3, 2022, https://www.catholicleague.org/5-of-voters-support-no-limits-on-abortion/.

[41] Michael W. Chapman, "K of C/Marist Poll: 69% of Americans Support Limiting Abortion to at Least 3 Months of Pregnancy," CNS News, January 18, 2023, https://cnsnews.com/article/national/michael-w-chapman/kofcmarist-poll-69-americans-support-limiting-abortion-least#.

[42] "America's Abortion Quandary," Pew Research Center, May 6, 2022, 8, https://www.pewresearch.org/religion/wp-content/uploads/sites/7/2022/05/PF_05.06.22_abortion.views_.full-report.pdf.

example, 81 percent who say religion is "extremely important to their views" say abortion should generally be illegal. By contrast, 87 percent who say religion is not important to them believe that abortion should be legal in most situations. The vast majority of religious Americans also say doctors should be required to notify parents of minors before an abortion, but the majority of atheists and agnostics disagree.[43]

The moral divide becomes even more interesting when we compare views on abortion and the death penalty. In the Pew survey, almost 100 percent of atheists (97 percent) believe that abortion should be legal,[44] but in a Pew survey taken a year earlier, it found that two in three atheists (65 percent) oppose the death penalty (a majority of religious Americans favor the death penalty).[45]

How can this be? Abortion, which is commonplace, is the taking of innocent human life; the death penalty, which is uncommon, is imposed on those found guilty of the most serious crimes. It seems bizarre that atheists, who do not recognize the rights of the unborn, are quite sensitive about the rights of serial killers.

This outcome can be explained, at least in part, by considering that atheists are the most likely segment of society to believe that abortion should not be considered a moral

[43] Ibid., 46, 69.
[44] Ibid., 30.
[45] Stephanie Kramer, "Unlike Other U.S. Religious Groups, Most Atheists and Agnostics Oppose the Death Penalty," Pew Research Center, June 15, 2021, https://www.pewresearch.org/fact-tank/2021/06/15/unlike-other-religious-groups-most-atheists-and-agnostics-oppose-the-death-penalty/.

issue: 37 percent compared to 21 percent overall (religious Americans are the most likely to see abortion as a moral issue).[46] To understand how anyone can declare abortion not to be a moral issue, it is instructive to understand the meaning of natural law.

NATURAL LAW

How do we know anything is morally wrong rather than simply a difference of opinion? If opinion is all that matters, and if we are ruled by a democratic majority, shouldn't the most popular moral opinion be enshrined in law? What if those who favor slavery are in the majority? Should they have the moral right to impose their views on the rest of society? As long as no one is required to own a slave, on what grounds should those who oppose slavery object? On what moral basis can we privilege one moral code over another?

When Nazis were put on trial at Nuremberg, they defended the killing of innocent Jews by saying they were only following orders. Indeed, they *were* following orders, but they were still convicted. Nevertheless, on what basis? Not only were they subject to a chain of command, but what they did was also legal in their own country when they did it. What law could possibly have been invoked against them?

The answer is the natural law, which is comprised of objective truths about right and wrong that have been perceived across cultures and across civilizations. The law that the Nazis were following is known as the positive law — that

---

[46] "America's Abortion Quandary," 50.

is, the law that the government posits. But the Nuremberg courts ruled that the Nazis had to know in their hearts that to intentionally kill innocent Jews was wrong, no matter what they were told. "The positive legislative act," one court said, "is intrinsically limited. It loses all obligatory power if it violates the generally recognized principles of international law or the natural law, or if the contradiction between the positive law and justice reaches such an intolerable degree that the law ... must give way to justice."[47]

We know from reason and experience that there are some basic acts that are inherently immoral. Of course, many aspects of life — culinary preferences, music selections, favorite sports teams — do not concern the moral law. There are no objectively right or wrong answers to these questions. But when it comes to moral questions, questions about right and wrong, the natural law is the highest law.

It was on the basis of natural law principles that slavery was outlawed. In his famous debates with Stephen Douglas in 1858, Abraham Lincoln appealed to the natural law in making the case against slavery. He did so by invoking the Declaration of Independence. Five years later, when he gave his Gettysburg Address, he made the same observation, namely that "all men are created equal." It was empirically obvious to Douglas, and to every defender of slavery, that black people were human beings, even though they weren't being treated that way. It did not matter that they were called chattel or cattle. It did not matter that democratic

---

[47] Charles E. Rice, *50 Questions on the Natural Law* (San Francisco: Ignatius Press, 1993), 26.

majorities had enshrined slavery in the law. Everyone really knew that slaves were as human as their masters.

In the West, Aristotle is considered the "father of natural law" (though he himself did not use the term). He said that there were some acts that all human beings know are morally wrong. Similarly, Cicero maintained that "right is based, not upon men's opinions, but upon Nature."[48] But it was Thomas Aquinas who expanded our understanding of natural law by offering a Christian account of it. He wrote that the natural law was grounded in the eternal law, which is to say in God Himself. The natural law, he said, was to be understood within the context of the divine law, or the law as found in the Old and New Testaments. In fact, the natural law is reflected in the moral tenets of the Old Testament. Natural law, Aquinas taught, is but "a participation by rational creatures in the eternal law," which means it is part of divine providence.[49]

If everyone knows that there are some acts that are wrong, how is it that people can commit horrendous crimes? How can they ignore the natural law? Aquinas teaches that it is possible for us to blot out the natural law, particularly by repeated acts of evil.[50] In other words, we can sideline our conscience by constantly committing very serious sinful acts. This bears resemblance to what Hannah

[48]   Ibid., 35.
[49]   Francis Selman, *Aquinas 101: A Basic Introduction to the Thought of Saint Thomas Aquinas* (Notre Dame, IN: Ave Maria Press, 2005), 139.
[50]   Rice, *Natural Law*, 59.

Arendt said about the Nazis: she called this phenomenon "the banality of evil."

If the teachings of Aquinas were confined to the classroom and intellectual discussions, their impact on society might be limited. But they are not limited to abstract discussions. When Rev. Martin Luther King Jr. was imprisoned in Birmingham, Alabama, he wrote his famous letter, drawing on Aquinas: "A just law is a man-made code that squares with the moral law or the law of God. . . . An unjust law is a code that is out of harmony with the moral law. To put it in the terms of Saint Thomas Aquinas: 'An unjust law is a human law that is not rooted in eternal and natural law.'"[51]

THE TELEOLOGICAL NATURE OF NATURAL LAW

In addition to providing a foundation for right and wrong, the natural law—for those who believe in it—suggests that life itself has a purpose. Right and wrong do not simply exist for no reason. They have a goal, an end, or *telos*, for which society, and indeed the universe, exists.

Karin Öberg teaches astronomy at Harvard University. The Swedish-born scientist also serves on the board of the international Society of Catholic Scientists, and she believes that we live in a universe that "has a beginning, a middle, and an end that's unfolding over time." She says that belief in God helps scientists because it provides a "sure foundation" for understanding the universe. She notes that the

[51] Ibid., 28.

author of the big bang theory of the universe, Georges Lemaître, was a priest, and that his work is now considered the conventional wisdom in scientific circles. "I can't help but wonder if ... the reason that he had the idea, instead of some of the other brilliant scientists that he was surrounded by, had something to do with his Catholicism," she says.[52]

Öberg, a former atheist, challenges the popular notion that we can only know if something is true by relying on science. Science is certainly one way to learn about some truths. But she contends that there are many aspects of truth, and many ways of discovering them. For example, she says, when it comes to moral issues, religion and philosophy provide reasons for our understanding that science simply does not and cannot provide.

The teleology, or end purpose, of the law is to bring about the common good. Christians and Jews who believe in the God of the Bible believe that by following His will, as outlined in the Ten Commandments, we can form a good society. To secularists, however, this is folly. They favor an individualistic conception of morality that allows individuals to choose what, if any, norms they should obey. The clash of cultures could not be more stark.

The religious vision inclines toward a society with a natural order of being, including the existence of a flexible but fixed human nature. For example, as human beings we

---

[52] Jonah McKeown, "Harvard Scientist: The Wonders of the Universe Point to a Creator," *Catholic News Agency*, January 21, 2023, catholicnewsagency.com/news/253394/harvard-scientist-the-wonders-of-the-universe-point-to-a-creator.

were meant to live with others in community; accordingly, we must learn to subordinate, sometimes, our self-interest to the best interests of society. We must respect the social institutions of marriage and the family, and jealously guard against attempts to subvert them.

The secular vision of society accepts the Enlightenment view that society is composed of aggregates of individuals. The law, according to this perspective, is optimally designed to promote the rights of the individual, rather than the overarching common good.

Society is not merely a bunch of individuals. Human beings are naturally social. Human society is naturally comprised of groups—families, kinship groups, tribes, clans, parishes, communities, organizations—all of which form a reality that transcends the many individuals who live within its normative boundaries.

The idea that morality can be dissolved to individual claims is not simply wrong; it is pernicious. For example, no one could drive to school or work unless a moral code was understood and enforced. We don't leave it to each driver to determine what is right and wrong, and that's why we have lights, signs, and lines on the road. Society is based on a consensus of what is right and wrong. Those notions can change over time, but there can never be a situation without a general agreement of what is right and wrong.

Everyone agrees that a free society must have respect for civil liberties, or the rights of the individual. We must also acknowledge, however, that there are needs that society must fulfill, among them being a modicum of civility and community, without which there is social decomposition.

Here's the rub. Civil liberties are predicated on the rights of the individual prevailing over the will of the majority. Civility and community, on the other hand, are predicated on the will of the majority prevailing over the rights of the individual. A mature society will acknowledge the competing nature of these desires and strike a balance. Our current moral and civil crisis is largely the result of our preoccupation with the rights of the individual at the expense of society, of civility, and of community. The extreme idea that every man, woman, and child should be able to maintain his or her own personal morality — and that society should nevertheless be able to function smoothly — is simply mad.

CONSENT AND REASON AS THE BASIS OF MORALITY

Not all secularists promote such extremes of personal morality. Most secularists try to ground morality in such a way that certain norms continue to prevail. These secularists believe that consent and reason can provide the basis for a common morality.

Consent is indeed an important moral attribute in any philosophical system that values freedom. But alone, it is inadequate to the task. For example, bribery is consensual. But the effects of bribery are not limited to those who are party to it. That is why it is illegal.

If consent is all that is needed to make an act moral, consent can justify incest. If the mother and the son agree to have sex, who can object? What law does it break? The natural law, for one. In addition, for believers it violates the eternal law (God's wisdom) and the divine law (Scripture) that undergird the natural law. Yet secularists cannot avail themselves of these constraints on morality to condemn incest. It is true, a secularist could say that reason, rather than consent, prohibits incest because incest tends to result, over time, in unhealthy offspring. But that is a prudential consideration. It does not provide a foundation for saying that the act itself is morally wrong.

Notwithstanding these objections, the contemporary idea of morality, as understood by our elites and accepted by millions, is that everything goes as long as it is consensual. This conception of morality finds its roots in John Stuart Mill's 1859 book-length essay, *On Liberty*, where Mill enunciated his "one very simple principle"—namely, that "the sole end for which mankind are warranted, individually or collectively, in interfering with the liberty of action of any of their number is self-protection." To be sure that we get his point, Mill adds that "the only purpose for which power can be rightfully exercised over any member of a civilized community, against his will, is to prevent harm to others."[53]

On paper, Mill's idea sounds plausible. In real life, it's a mess—and it leads to needless suffering for many individuals. For example, the logic of Mill's thought implies that society has no legitimate right to protect individuals even

[53] Bill Donohue, "Consent Alone Is No Basis for Morality," Catholic League," October 27, 1998, https://catholicleague. org/consent-alone-is-no-basis-for-morality.

from their self-destruction; it would also challenge legal restrictions on pornography, prostitution, gambling, narcotics,
and the like.

Right now many American cities are overrun by drugs.
Children go to school and adults go to work walking
through a civic minefield, shuffling around men and women
who are totally out of their minds. Some are mentally ill;
they harass passersby; they defecate in the streets; they shoot
up in public. We rescue cats and dogs who have strayed and
are in need. But our idolization of the individual impels us
to ignore human beings who are in great need. Living on the
streets is not liberating—it is dehumanizing.

Idolizing individualism also invariably means favoring
some individuals while diminishing the rights of others. We
have forgotten why we have laws on pornography and prostitution. They were written as much to protect the family as
to prosecute prostitutes. Men, much more than women, are
given to sexual temptations; they can be tempted to stray
unless they are encouraged to practice self-discipline. Pornography and prostitution lure men and lead them to
objectify sex and women. Gambling attacks the family as
well. It allows men—some of whom are, by nature, given to
risk-taking—to take chances that statistically backfire (the
house always wins). Some men become addicted to gambling, which places the financial well-being of their wives
and children in jeopardy. That's why it is regulated.

In 1874, philosopher James Fitzjames Stephen answered
Mill, saying, "The condition of human life is such that we
must of necessity be restricted and compelled by circumstances

in nearly every action of our lives." He then raised a key question: "Why, then, is liberty, defined as Mr. Mill defines it, to be regarded as so precious?"[54]

The fundamental tension between Mill and Stephen lay in their view of society. Mill saw individuals—walking, talking, eating, working, playing—all going about their life alone. He saw no groups, just masses of individuals. Stephen had a different vision: "A man would no more be a man if he was alone in the world than a hand would be a hand without the rest of the body."[55] In short, for Stephen, the individual is only intelligible as he is connected to others.

Intellectuals living in the eighteenth century believed they were living in the "age of reason" so impressed were they by advances in science and technology. But they made too much of it. Many things are difficult to see under the microscope of pure reason, such as love and beauty.

For example, from the perspective of the rationalist, funerals make no sense. The dead cannot appreciate the love or mourning of their friends and family, so why bother? If the mourning is done for the living, why do they have to go to such expense? For what reason do people save the ashes of the dead? What are they going to do with them? Why do people enlist to join the armed forces, putting their own lives at risk to protect people they don't know? How does this make any sense?

Why do people save heirlooms? To remember the dead? But why remember them? They are gone and not coming back. Why do people want the autograph of a famous person?

[54] Ibid.
[55] Ibid.

What utility does it serve? Why do people pay exorbitant amounts of money to buy a baseball or a football possessed by a great player? Why do fans buy the player's jersey? What are they going to do with it? Why buy artwork, or collect stamps, or do any of the myriad other things that bring joy to people, but make no sense to rationalists.

Life would be very dull if every human act had to pass the acid test of reason. More important, if reason is our only guide to morality—which is the dream of secularists—the world would be a nightmare.

On the basis of reason alone, how would it be possible to ban sadomasochism? If John offers to pay Joe to beat him with a whip in public, what reason could be given to forbid it?

On the basis of reason alone, how would it be possible to ban a duel to the death between two consenting adults? If the public wants to watch it on TV, on what basis could the will of the public be denied?

On the basis of reason alone, how would it be possible to ban bestiality? If Fred wants to have sex with Fido, is it not his right to do so?

On the basis of reason alone, how would it be possible to ban the sale of fentanyl? If that is what makes some people happy, who are we to stop them from doing so?

On the basis of reason alone, how would it be possible to ban prostitution? If a woman agrees to sell her body to a man, why should they not have the right to do so?

On the basis of reason alone, how would it be possible to ban public nudity? If some people enjoy going naked in the street, on what basis should we deprive them of such a right?

Why is it considered indecent for a man to expose himself? His genitals are part of his body, just like his hands and his ears. Why do we allow people to expose their hands and ears but not their genitals? If some are offended, why can't they avert their eyes?

Secularists who rely on consent and reason as the basis for morality would have to permit these behaviors. Indeed, many no doubt would—some with pleasure. Some, undoubtedly, would balk and feel uneasy about legalizing such acts. But that is not a reason. It's a feeling. And a society that allows feelings to be the basis of its moral code is playing with fire. What happens when someone feels like they have a right to take your life?

Fortunately, we have not yet reached the stage where reason alone reigns. So on what basis do we ban these behaviors? Some Supreme Court rulings are instructive.

In *Paris Adult Theatre I v. Slaton* (1973), the high court ruled in an obscenity case that there is a legitimate state interest in morality. "In an unbroken series of cases extending over a long stretch of this Court's history it has been accepted as a postulate that 'the primary requirements of decency may be enforced against obscene publications.'"[56]

It also detailed what underlies the state's interest in morality, listing "the interest of the public in the quality of life and the total community environment, the tone of commerce in the great city centers, and, possibly, the public safety itself....

---

[56] Daniel F. Piar, "Morality as a Legitimate Government Interest," *Penn State Law Review* 117, no. 1 (2012): 148.

As Chief Justice Warren stated, there is a 'right of the Nation and of the States to maintain a decent society.'"[57]

If the "quality of life" and "the total community environment" matter as a means of maintaining "a decent society," then behaviors that contravene these ends cannot be countenanced, not even in the name of freedom of expression.

To put it more plainly, laws against indecent exposure need to be upheld because the maintenance of a decent society is conditioned on a respect for modesty, which is a natural human trait. The sexual organs are covered in public because they are manifestly not like our hands and ears: when stimulated, they may be recklessly exercised. That is one reason why marriage is a universal institution: every society in history has found it necessary to constructively channel the sex drive so that it is not exercised in a promiscuous fashion. It is precisely because sexual acts may lead to procreation that society has an interest in regulating it. In short, indecent exposure laws protect the moral order, and are thus in the best interests of society.

Everyone understands the need to guard against air and water pollution. When it spreads, it can endanger the community. The same is true of moral pollution. When it spreads, it endangers us all.

[57] Ibid.

CHAPTER 2

DENYING TRUTH

DENYING TRUTH HAS CONSEQUENCES

PHILOSOPHERS THROUGHOUT THE AGES have quarreled about what constitutes a good society and how to achieve it. But to many of today's intellectuals, such concerns seem quaint. They have reached a stage of exhaustion and resignation. They seem more interested in tearing down society than in understanding or improving it. The Enlightenment interest in reason, science, and the creation of responsible liberal values has faded. A decadent postmodernism has replaced it.

We can thank the French for planting the seeds of post-modern thinking. Beginning in the 1960s, French intellectuals turned sharply left, questioning the value—even the existence—of virtually every aspect of society, including truth itself. They embarked on a nihilistic journey that has led every Western nation down a dark path.

The postmodernist conception of reality is radical. Indeed, postmodernism represents the most extreme expression of secular morality. Its proponents assert that what we think exists is actually only a matter of our perceptions. They do not believe in objective morality. To them, right and wrong are simply social constructs, codes that reflect the preferences of the ruling elite with no intrinsic worth.

This is moral nihilism. Instead of learning from the wisdom of the ages, today's postmodern intellectuals satisfy themselves with deconstruction. The great intellectual discoveries of the Western world as recorded in our great books are reduced to an author's identity and social standing. The text doesn't matter; only biography matters. Nothing is sacred— except perhaps the thoughts of postmodern intellectuals.

Thankfully, there are some writers who have not intoxicated themselves on the spirits of postmodern thinking. A few brave souls continue to stand for the truth, and try to showcase the absurdity of postmodern thinking. Alan Sokal is one of them.

Sokal is a physicist who got fed up with hearing nonsense about truth not existing. In 1996, he submitted an article to an academic journal, *Social Text*, that was known as "a leading North American journal of cultural studies." Sokal's article contended that gravity was a "social construct," which had nothing to do with nature. The journal's scholars were enthralled by his work and published it eagerly—at which point Sokal exposed them for the fools they were by announcing it was a hoax. He just wanted to test their gullibility. Naturally, they vilified him, rather than eating their humble pie.[58]

---

[58] Quoted in John Podhoretz, "The Latest Lunatic Postmodern Target: Motherhood," *New York Post*, May 12, 2015, https://

In 2018, a trio of authors was revealed to have submitted twenty articles to peer-reviewed journals that were also pure bunk. Under a variety of pseudonyms, they dressed their language up in classic postmodern style. Guess what? Four articles were published.[59]

David Detmer is a philosopher who reveals the preposterousness of postmodern writers. He interviewed one of them, fellow philosopher Laurie Calhoun. On the record, he asked Calhoun a simple question that any preschool child could answer: whether giraffes are taller than ants. No, she replied, it is "an article of religious faith in our culture."[60]

This is what happens when postmodernism sinks it. It disables the ability to reason. That people like this are working in the academy, instead of being housed in an asylum, is a national disgrace.

St. John Paul II rightly observed that "some philosophers have abandoned the search for truth and made their sole aim the attainment of a subjective certainty or a pragmatic sense of utility. This, in turn, has obscured the true dignity of reason."[61] In his magnificent encyclical *Veritatis*

nypost.com/2015/05/12/the-latest-lunatic-postmodern-target-motherhood/.

59 Bill Donohue, *Common Sense Catholicism: How to Resolve Our Cultural Crisis* (San Francisco: Ignatius Press, 2019), 104.

60 Helen Pluckrose, "How French 'Intellectuals' Ruined the West: Postmodernism and Its Impact, Explained," *Areo*, March 27, 2017, https://areomagazine.com/2017/03/27/how-french-intellectuals-ruined-the-west-postmodernism-and-its-impact-explained/.

61 Charles E. Rice, *50 Questions on the Natural Law* (San Francisco: Ignatius Press, 1993), 41–42.

Splendor, he begins by saying, "The splendor of truth shines forth in all the works of the Creator and, in a special way, in man, created in the image and likeness of God. Truth enlightens man's intelligence and shapes his freedom, leading him to know and love the Lord." He also noted that salvation would be had by "obedience to the truth."[62]

The idea that truth is a means to freedom, and that salvation is achieved by obedience to truth, is baffling to those with a secular vision of man and society (and especially to postmodern philosophers). And consider the irony. The Catholic Church is looked upon with disbelief by the same secular intellectuals who themselves proclaim the most wild and fanciful ideas.

John Paul II identified the fruit of postmodern-ism — nihilism. Nihilism, he said, is a "philosophy of nothingness," which, he notes, "has a certain attraction for people of our time." Its adherents have no "hope or possibility of ever attaining the goal of truth. In the nihilist interpretation, life is no more than an occasion for sensations and experiences in which the ephemeral has pride of place." What exists, according to this conception, is the belief that "everything is fleeting and provisional." This, he says, is at the heart of nihilism, which has become a "widespread mentality."[63]

---

[62] John Paul II, encyclical letter *Veritatis Splendor* (August 6, 1993), https://www.vatican.va/content/john-paul-ii/en/encyclicals/documents/hf_jp_ii_enc_06081993_veritatis-splendor.html.

[63] Rice, *Natural Law*, 42.

Things have deteriorated even since John Paul II offered these insights. In 2016, the *Oxford English Dictionary* chose "post-truth" as its "word of the year." It defined it as "relating to or denoting circumstances in which objective facts are less influential in shaping public opinion than appeals to emotion and personal belief."[64]

Consider that it is not at all uncommon to hear commentators on TV ask their guests to explain "your truth," as if truth (rather than experience) can vary from one person to another. Such nonsense used to be confined to the couches of therapists; it is now the preferred parlance of the chattering class.

The late Jonathan Sacks, a brilliant English rabbi and philosopher, noted a few years ago "the loss of truth as a value." This is particularly true among intellectuals. "There is no such thing as truth, goes the postmodern mantra; there are only interpretations. There is no such thing as history; there are only narratives." The university, he observed, "is no longer seen as a community of scholars in pursuit of truth; instead it is viewed as a system of power."[65] Obsessed with tales of inequality and oppression, the big minds are empty people, constantly looking for relief from their own unhappiness. So despondent are they that they are even the subject of a book on this subject by Eddie Scarry, *Liberal Misery: How the Hateful Left Sucks Joy out of Everything and Everyone.* And in a 2022 poll, liberals were 18 percentage points less

[64] Jonathan Sacks, *Morality: Restoring the Common Good in Divided Times* (New York: Basic Books, 2020), 160.
[65] Ibid., 179.

likely to say they were happy with life as compared to conservatives.[66]

Sacks is right. The university is "no longer seen as a community of scholars in pursuit of truth." I had a chance to champion this point when I debated John Coatsworth, dean of Columbia University's School of International and Public Affairs, about the propriety of hosting Mahmoud Ahmadinejad, the Iranian president, in 2007. The exchange took place on the *Today* show.

"A university does believe in freedom of speech, but freedom of speech is a means to an end," I said. "The end of a university is the pursuit of truth. It's a normative community." What disqualifies the Iranian dictator, I insisted, is his conviction that "the Holocaust did not exist." I accused him of "spitting in the face of every Jew in New York City. That is a demonstrably false idea."

When asked by Matt Lauer if Ahmadinejad should be allowed to speak, I answered, "He should be allowed to speak. He should go to a forum which doesn't represent anything, such as Madison Square Garden. A university is not about freedom of speech. If Columbia believes that freedom of speech is the highest virtue, why the hell did they not allow the founder of the Minutemen to speak there two weeks ago? That's because they found his speech objectionable. A university is engaged in the pursuit of truth. Any rational person will understand that Ahmadinejad has no

[66] W. Bradford Wilcox, "Why Are Liberals Less Happy than Conservatives?," UnHerd, October 10, 2022, https://unherd.com/thepost/why-are-liberals-less-happy-than-conservatives/.

legitimate platform. The dean says he's not sure, we can't make judgments in advance." I closed by saying, "I think you ought to retire, sir."[67]

Richard Rorty, the American postmodern philosopher, rejects all notions of objective truth. For instance, Rorty sneers at those who say that the artistic, scientific, technological, economic, and intellectual achievements of Western civilization are superior to other civilizations on the grounds that no objective yardstick exists to make such a judgment. For him, such a claim is not only illegitimate, but it smacks of hubris. The concept of truth, objectivity, and reality that undergirds typical Western thinking, he says, is not to be taken seriously.

I encountered his kind of thinking when I gave a speech in the 1980s before students who were working on their Ph.D.s in engineering at Carnegie Mellon University. Two students were offended by my defense of the West—and of America, in particular—so I asked them if they believed that all cultures and civilizations were morally equal. They smirked and said of course they were. I wanted to make sure I understood them correctly, so I said, "In this country we put pizzas into ovens, and in Hitler's Germany they put Jews into ovens. Different strokes for different folks, right?" The smile was wiped off their faces. They nervously mumbled, "That is not what we mean." But I explained, "That is exactly what you

[67] The transcript is available on LexisNexis, "Many Object to Iranian President Mahmoud Ahmadinejad Speaking at Columbia University; John Coatsworth, Dean of Columbia's School of International and Public Affairs, and Bill Donohue, President of the Catholic League, Discuss Subject," *Today*, September 24, 2007.

mean—what I said follows logically from what you said." Ideas matter; and principles matter. I suggested that they might want to rethink theirs.

To be fair, they were only students who had absorbed the ideas of postmodern professors. It is the leftist intellectuals themselves who are really to blame.

Some writers contend that the denial of the existence of truth is traceable to Nietzsche. But Nietzsche did not deny the reality of truth as much as he questioned its importance. Yet even he acknowledged that when truth dies, we are left with nothing but the will to power. So if truth is unimportant, and there is no arbitrator of right and wrong, then the strong win. The pursuit of power fills the vacuum, and that portends a grim future.

MORAL RELATIVISM

The idea that there is no objective standard of morality is appealing not only to intellectuals but to millions of Americans who are preoccupied with satisfying their own passions and interests. To them, being nonjudgmental is the highest virtue because it allows for maximum autonomy and freedom.

But to those interested in crafting a good society, freedom and autonomy are not ends. They are important elements that indeed have a role to play. But they serve morality—and goodness—and must be subordinated to it.

Time magazine named Albert Einstein the person of the twentieth century—and then credited his theory of relativity with spawning moral relativism. Einstein's theory, though, explained in physical terms how time and space were not absolute things but were in fact related to each other. He said nothing, in professional terms, about morality. But as historian Paul Johnson put it, "Mistakenly but perhaps inevitably, relativity became confused with relativism."[68]

However, Einstein was a physicist, not a philosopher — and he was no moral relativist. According to Johnson, while Einstein was a nonpracticing Jew, he did acknowledge the existence of God. Furthermore, "he believed passionately in absolute standards of right and wrong. His professional life was devoted to the quest not only of truth but for certitude."[69]

Isaiah Berlin, the distinguished philosopher, concurs. "The word relativity has been widely misunderstood as relativism, the denial, or doubt about, the objectivity of truth or moral values. This was the opposite of what Einstein believed. He was a man of simple and absolute moral convictions, which were expressed in all he was and did."[70]

The rise of moral relativism took root in the waning days of the Middle Ages and sprouted during the Enlightenment. In essence, it became the new paganism. Morality was no longer anchored in God's will; it was anchored in human feelings and emotions.

David Hume did more than anyone to promote this subjectivist philosophy. He argued that pain and pleasure,

---

[68] Paul Johnson, *Modern Times: The World from the Twenties to the Eighties* (New York: Harper & Row, 1983), 4.

[69] Ibid.

[70] Al Mohler, "Relativity, Moral Relativism, and the Modern Age," *The Aquila Report*, https://theaquilareport.com/relativity-moral-relativism-and-the-modern-age/.

rather than right and wrong, were at the heart of moral decisions. That which gives us pleasure is good, and that which results in pain is bad. The appeal of this simple philosophy is easy to understand, especially for those who loath Judeo-Christian morality. But its ability to govern a purposeful life, rather than a selfish life, is understandably limited.

In the nineteenth century, Charles Darwin argued that there was no such thing as a universal morality that was understood by men in every culture. Thus, he denied the existence of natural law and held that our conceptions of morality were simply accidents of natural selection. For example, he cited infanticide and suicide as common practices in history that were not seen as immoral, and he did so in a very clinical, nonjudgmental fashion.

Karl Marx also believed that morality had no independent reality, arguing that moral codes are nothing more than "phantoms formed in the human brain." No wonder he believed that truth was only that which serves the cause. Perhaps it is not surprising that those who most operationalized his views turned into mass murderers. They had no reason to think they were doing anything wrong.

In the twentieth century, postmodernists, especially in France, challenged every traditional understanding of morality. Jacques Derrida took aim at the belief that there is a final external authority. He was also the father of deconstruction, a school of thought that originated in France in the 1960s. He questioned the idea that there are inherent meanings, even to the point of challenging the belief that words mean what the author says they mean. In other words, because there are no truths, the world is a fiction.

Similarly, Michel Foucault, the postmodernist French scholar, contends that there is no objective means, or principles, of determining the truth. We are so enmeshed in our culture, he says, that we do not possess the ability to transcend it; thus, what we perceive as true is simply a cultural idea. Indeed, what we regard as knowledge is nothing more than a social construct. Like those of virtually all postmodernists, Foucault's writings are so vague and incoherent that it is often hard to understand what their point is. I am convinced that they like it that way—it gives them a way out when challenged.

Postmodernism elevated moral relativism to new heights. Society is not held together by a moral consensus, its practitioners said. Rather, it is held together only by power and oppression. Where there are hierarchies, they argue—including moral hierarchies—there is oppression. Given this mindset, we can see why these big thinkers are so attracted to nihilism: they wish to destroy in the name of freedom.

But this idolizing of freedom, like the pursuit of all idols, ends in misery. No Catholic understood this better than Pope Benedict XVI. He was not only a brilliant philosopher, but he also possessed a keen sociological mind. On the day before he was chosen to be the bishop of Rome, Cardinal Joseph Ratzinger delivered his classic homily on the "dictatorship of relativism." By that he meant the consequences of rejecting moral absolutes: it leaves the individual as the ultimate measure of right and wrong. That has severe consequences for society, he counseled, and this is especially true when young people reject moral absolutes.

What Benedict said about young people is confirmed by survey data. In 2021, a survey of young people found that four in ten millennials (those born between 1981 and 1996) said they either didn't know, didn't care, or didn't believe that God exists. Three-quarters of teens and young adults said that what is "morally right and wrong changes over time."[71] On one level, this is true, but there is a profound difference between treating this as a historical observation and treating it as a worthy social compass. Given this state of mind, it is not surprising to learn that a Harvard study released in 2022 showed that young people reported having the lowest life satisfaction scores of any age group.[72] The "dictatorship of relativism" is everywhere apparent. For example, those who do not accept the secular vision of marriage, the family, and sexuality promoted by moral relativism know exactly how intolerant moral relativists can be.

When the Little Sisters of the Poor are told they must pay for abortion-inducing drugs in their healthcare plans, this is an example of intolerance, not tolerance. When Catholic doctors and hospitals are told they must perform abortions and sex-reassignment surgeries, this is a vile expression of intolerance. When priests are arrested for praying

[71] Alvin Powell, "Why Are Young People So Miserable?," *Harvard Gazette*, September 15, 2022, https://news.harvard.edu/gazette/story/2022/09/why-are-young-people-so-miserable/.

[72] Ibid.

outside an abortion clinic, what could be more intolerant? When those who hold to a traditional understanding of marriage are subjected to ridicule and derision, there is nothing tolerant about that. When school therapists encourage children to transition to the other sex—behind the backs of their parents—this is intolerance personified.

Matters get worse when relativism is orchestrated by the nation-state. "If relativism signifies contempt for fixed categories and [for] men who claim to be bearers of an external objective truth, then there is nothing more relativistic than fascist attitudes."[73] So said Benito Mussolini. But bad as he was, Stalin, Hitler, and Mao raised totalitarianism to new heights. They denied the existence of truth and moral absolutes—and their regimes caused the deaths of approximately 150 million people.

To those who say that Christians also have blood on their hands, it must be said, yes indeed, there have certainly been Christians—and even Christian states—that have committed murder and theft and every other sin. However, these atrocities were done in *violation* of Christian tenets. Those who killed in the name of Communism did not violate its tenets; if anything, they complied with the dictates of their secular philosophy.

Cardinal George Pell understood the threat of relativism, but he was not convinced it had a future. "One reason for optimism is that no one believes deep down in relativism.

---

[73] Roger Kimball, "Introduction: The Dictatorship of Relativism," *New Criterion*, January 2009, www.newcriterion.com/issues/2009/1/introduction-the-dictatorship-of-relativism.

People may express their skepticism about truth and morality in lecture rooms or in print, but afterwards, they will go on to sip a cappuccino, pay the mortgage, drive home on the left side of the road, and presumably avoid acts of murder and cannibalism throughout their evening. People, unless insane, do not live as relativists."[74]

It is true that those who espouse relativist ideas rarely live as relativists. But that is of little consequence to those impacted by laws, and social policies, that express relativist ideas. Relativist ideas, like all ideas, have consequences— and Pell well understood the chaos wrought by them.

I witnessed many examples firsthand when I was a professor. At a faculty meeting, I remember some of my colleagues objecting to the idea that there was such a thing as correct spelling. They branded this idea "logocentrism," an antiquated idea born of moral certitude. I looked around the room and noticed that most of my peers appeared to have been swayed by this position. I couldn't let it go. I responded with a question: "So if the people who handle the payroll account misspell your name and address on your next check, does that mean you won't object?" That ended the discussion.

It is amazing to me how many highly educated people can be seduced by the silliest of ideas. It would be funny if it weren't so sad.

[74] Cardinal George Pell, "The Dictatorship of Relativism," EWTN, https://www.ewtn.com/catholicism/library/dictatorship-of-relativism-3931.

MARRIAGE, PROPERLY UNDERSTOOD

The highly individualist Enlightenment view of marriage and the family eventually found its way into American law. In many ways, it reflected the bleak, totalitarian vision of Rousseau: in his conception of society, there is only the individual and the state. The mediating institutions of the family, church, community organizations, voluntary associations, unions—the entities that integrate the individual into society, provide forums for purpose and meaning, and serve as a shield against the state—are all missing. As Tocqueville noted, these coalitions are the best guarantor of freedom we can establish. If the state is not kept at bay—and that is what these bonding agents do—the loss of freedom is inevitable.

The natural law tradition stands squarely against this radical secular vision. As Aquinas explained, society is not composed merely of autonomous individuals. There is a common good, something greater than the totality of individual interests and pursuits. Indeed, in Catholic teaching, it is the family, not the individual, that reigns supreme with respect to worldly matters. Pope John XXIII noted that the family is "the natural, primary cell of human society."[75] This truth is based on the anthropological reality that men and women are different and complementary and that reproduction depends on a man and a woman. For Aquinas, this is central to his philosophy—so much so that it is one of his three major precepts of

---

[75] John XXIII, encyclical letter *Pacem in Terris* (April 11, 1963), no. 16.

natural law. To be specific, the duty to propagate and care for offspring is of the highest importance.

This all sounds like basic common sense to many Americans. But to many others — including, most especially, well-educated secularists — it is disturbing. Their secular vision considers this elementary observation to be too exclusive, too prejudiced against alternative social models. Yet no one can deny that the human race is the product of the sexual union of men and women. Furthermore, the best way to raise children is in the intact family comprised of a mother and a father, and no amount of ideological chatter to the contrary can deny this verity — the social science evidence is overwhelming.

Catholic teaching insists that the state not supersede the family. Its role must always be subordinate. For instance, as St. John Paul II argued, if the family is to do its job of teaching charity, chastity, and other forms of religious instruction, then any intrusion by the state into these fundamental areas cannot be tolerated.

Harry Jaffa was not Catholic, but his exposition of natural law sounds very much like that of Aquinas. According to Jaffa, what makes men and women special is "the ability of two members of the same species to generate a third, that confirms them as members of the same species." He further stated that anything that undermines this basic fact of life, such as homosexuality, rape, incest, and adultery, must be rejected. Such acts are wrong because "they are inconsistent with the harmony and good order of the family, which is the foundation of all social harmony and social order, and thereby of all human happiness."[76]

Secularists condemned Jaffa when he wrote this in 1990. Today, it would be considered almost criminal to question the validity—indeed, the reality—of homosexual "marriage." But from a natural law perspective, the idea that marriage could be anything other than the union of man and woman is absurd.

In 2023, when Pete Buttigieg, the secretary of transportation, was questioned about his travel expenses, some of which were considered inappropriate, he responded by saying that other public officials have taken their spouses on official business trips. "Why is it any different when it's me and my husband?"[77]

But does Buttigieg really have a husband? Of course not. He may love his friend, Chasten. But Chasten can never be Pete's husband, or vice versa. Why not? Nature itself precludes the possibility.

It is true that Buttigieg's relationship has been recorded by the state, and that the state uses the word *marriage* to refer to it. But that is a legal fiction. The *Encyclopedia Britannica* defines a legal fiction as "a rule assuming as true something that is clearly false."[78] The idea that a man can have a husband is clearly false,

[76] Harry V. Jaffa, *Homosexuality and the Natural Law* (n.p.: Claremont Institute, 1990), 33–34.
[77] Bill Donohue, "Does Buttigieg Really Have a Husband?," Catholic League, January 17, 2023, www.catholicleague.org/does-buttigieg-really-have-a-husband/.
[78] Ibid.

whatever Buttigieg claims, whatever the state claims, whatever anyone claims to the contrary.

As mentioned, Aquinas wrote that reproduction is one of the three natural inclinations (the others being self-preservation and reason). Reproduction has been ordained by God through nature to be the exclusive attribute of a man and a woman. Marriage exists so that the sex drive of men and women can be constructively channeled to provide for stable families for the benefit of children.

Indeed, there is an anatomical goodness of fit to a man and a woman that permits them to become one flesh, and it is this union that allows them to reproduce. This is natural. Without male and female mating, the human race would cease to exist.

No man can have a husband any more than a man can bear a child. He can say he can—in the same way that he can say he menstruates—but that doesn't make it true. A stepfather can tell strangers that he is the father of his wife's children, but that doesn't make it true. If someone introduced his uncle to a stranger, saying, "This is my aunt Joe," no one would believe him. Those who have blue eyes can claim they have brown eyes, but that doesn't change reality. A left-handed person can claim to be right-handed, but observation tells us otherwise. Gorillas do not give birth to kangaroos.

Nature can be stubborn. It is not a social construct. It is fixed. If you run into a wall, you will get hurt, even if you believe the wall isn't there. The refusal to recognize reality harms society and the individuals caught up in madness.

So what should we call Chasten, if he is not Buttigieg's husband? His partner. His friend. His lover. The two of them may not like it, but truth is not determined by what is popular. It is determined by reality.

At bottom, people like Buttigieg refuse to accept that there is a natural world created by God. In 2023, the Committee on Doctrine of the U.S. bishops' conference issued a splendid statement on this subject: "A fundamental tenet of the Christian faith is that there is an order in the natural world that was designed by its Creator and this created order is good." Moreover, they said, "there is an order in human nature that we are called to respect."[79] Amen.

THE LAW AND RADICAL AUTONOMY

The legal antecedents to the recent wave of Supreme Court decisions restructuring the legal definitions of marriage, the family, and sexuality can be traced to the 1992 ruling in *Planned Parenthood v. Casey. Casey* reaffirmed the decision in *Roe v. Wade* that created the "right" of a woman to terminate her pregnancy prior to viability. But it was the remarkable reasoning of Justice Anthony Kennedy, who coauthored the majority opinion, that was most outrageous.

Kennedy wrote, "At the heart of liberty is the right to define one's own concept of existence, of meaning, of the

---

[79] Committee on Doctrine, U.S. Conference of Catholic Bishops, "Doctrinal Note on the Moral Limits to Technological Manipulation of the Human Body," March 20, 2023, https://www.usccb.org/resources/Doctrinal%20Note%202023-03-20.pdf.

universe, and of the mystery of life."[80] This sweeping declaration has nothing to do with constitutional law, or with
marriage, but it was the most pernicious, and unforgetta-
ble, line in his opinion. According to Kennedy, freedom
meant that each individual should choose why he exists
and assign whatever meaning he wants to his existence. He
can even define the universe anyway he wants. Ditto for
the "mystery of life," whatever that means. Kennedy's musings represent subjectivism in its most extreme
manifestation. I don't know if Kennedy ever read a single
book that denies the existence of truth — but he went to a
lot of elite universities and probably did. In any case, he
became infused with postmodernism and in fact became
the judicial poster boy for it.

From a Catholic perspective, Kennedy's exaltation of
the individual is not only ridiculous, but it also undercuts
the relationship between man and God. Pope Benedict
XVI did not mince words: "We can only be redeemed — that
is, we can only be free and true — if we stop wanting to be
a god, when we renounce our delusions of autonomy and
self-sufficiency."[81] In other words, we must establish a relationship with God if we are to be saved, and nothing
inhibits this more than to declare ourselves autonomous
human beings.

[80] *Planned Parenthood of Southeastern Pa. v. Casey*, 505 U.S. 833
(1992).
[81] Joseph Ratzinger (Benedict XVI), *The Divine Project: Reflections
on Creation and Church*, ed. Michael Langer and Karl-Heinz
Kronawetter, trans. Chase Faucheux (San Francisco: Ignatius
Press, 2022), 104.

But theology aside, the Court's ruling undermined many pillars of the law. In his dissent in *Casey*, Justice Antonin Scalia sarcastically noted, "The right to abort, we are told, inheres in 'liberty' because it is among 'a person's most basic decisions,'" one that involves "a most intimate and personal choic[e]."[82] He then explained that such reasoning could be used to justify a wide range of behaviors traditionally considered unacceptable. "Those adjectives might be applied, for example, to homosexual sodomy [which at the time was not entitled to constitutional protection], polygamy, adult incest, and suicide, all of which are equally 'intimate' and 'deep[ly] personal' decisions involving 'personal autonomy and bodily integrity,' and all of which can constitutionally be proscribed because it is our unquestionable constitutional tradition that they are proscribable." He then threw down the gavel: "It is not reasoned judgment that supports the Court's decision; only personal predilection."[83]

Scalia knew where the Supreme Court was headed. With this reasoning, it was only a matter of time before the high court overturned the 1986 decision in *Bowers v. Hardwick*, which concluded that the states had a right not to recognize the legality of homosexual behavior. In 2003, it did just that in *Lawrence v. Texas*. It is interesting to note that those who complained that overturning *Roe v. Wade* would unsettle "settled law" were cheering the unsettling of the longstanding law against sodomy. Respect for precedent

[82] *Planned Parenthood of Southeastern Pa. v. Casey.*
[83] Ibid.

seems not a matter of principle but only a tactical argument, conveniently invoked only when suited.

Instead of citing the reasoning employed by the courts throughout American history, the Supreme Court spoke emotionally about the way homosexuals were "demeaned" by laws making their behavior illicit. It is probably true that homosexual men and lesbians were upset by the law. But it is also true that many others whose behaviors are proscribed by law, such as prostitutes, feel abused by it. The law, however, serves to protect the community as a whole—which includes, for example, families and children. Therapeutic reasoning cannot provide a sound basis for constitutional law.

In his dissent in *Lawrence*, Scalia once again warned that acts traditionally considered to be so fundamentally immoral as to be proscribed by law were threatened by the decision to legalize homosexuality. After *Lawrence* was decided, I went on a CNN show hosted by Piers Morgan to debate this issue with a gay activist. Taking the same side as Scalia, I asked my adversary if he had any problem with legalizing incest. He refused to answer. Morgan pressed him, demanding an answer. He again refused. I explained that this was not a hypothetical question, and I cited the case of Allen and Patricia Muth, who had petitioned the court to allow them to marry. They are brother and sister. They relied on *Lawrence* to justify their "marriage." They lost their case, but it's not clear why. And future courts may well sanction incest. After all, the majority decision in *Lawrence* ended with the statement that the case did not sanction gay marriage. Twelve years later, another Supreme Court case did.

The American people never wanted to legalize gay marriage. Every time this issue was put to a vote in the states, the people voted against it. In the thirty states that had taken up this issue, the voters rejected same-sex marriage thirty times. Even in 2008, voters in the very liberal state of California affirmed the traditional meaning of marriage by rejecting same-sex marriage in Proposition 8. If gay activists and their elite supporters couldn't win in California, their chances of winning elsewhere seemed next to nil. The people had spoken.

But the elites didn't care what they thought. The 1960s line invoked by the Left, "Power to the People," was now rejected. Theodore Olson and David Boies—the two attorneys who had faced off against each other in the 2000 presidential race between George W. Bush and Al Gore—joined forces by challenging the position of Proposition 8 in the courts. It was a classic example of the elites versus the people.

In the Supreme Court oral arguments in *Obergefell v. Ohio*, Olson took a page from Justice Kennedy's decision in *Casey* and asserted the primacy of individual autonomy. He said marriage was a "personal right," not "society's right."[84] But societies do not have rights; they have only interests—and there are numerous societal interests involved in a legal definition of marriage that reflects the natural physical reality of reproduction through the pairing of men and

---

[84] Scott Shane, "Good Friends, Same Party but Legal Opponents," *New York Times*, March 26, 2013, https://www.nytimes.com/2013/03/27/us/politics/conservative-lawyers-are-opponents-on-gay-marriage.html.

women. By privatizing the social institution of marriage, Olson was making a sociologically incoherent argument.

Of course Olson and Boies won their case at the Supreme Court in 2015; and once again, Justice Kennedy, the apostle of radical individualism, wrote the majority opinion. But never once did Kennedy mention that the people of California had spoken clearly in rejecting Proposition 8. So much for democracy.

Drawing on his antisocial vision, he wrote that "a first premise of the Court's relevant precedents is that the right to personal choice regarding marriage is inherent in the concept of individual autonomy." Channeling *Casey*, he wrote about liberties that are "central to individual dignity and autonomy, including intimate choices that define personal identity and beliefs."[85] Nowhere in this absurd view of man and society is an awareness of the state's interests in the social order, or of the value and purpose of traditional moral strictures. It is the rule of the ego—what "I" want, I get.

From a historical perspective, the audacity of this decision is breathtaking. In one fell swoop, the Court declared that every state had been violating the Constitution all along by disallowing gay marriage. As Scalia observed, the contention was that all the great legal minds in Western history had had a blind spot, one that was finally corrected by the brilliance of today's justices.[86]

[85] *Obergefell et al. v. Hodges, Director, Ohio Department of Health, et al.*, 576 U.S. 644 (2015).
[86] Ibid.

The Court's arrogance is astounding, but no more than the obnoxious reasoning of Boies and Olson: When asked why they rushed to overturn Proposition 8, Olson said that someone was going to do it, so why not them? With characteristic bravado, he said, "We felt that if a challenge was going to be brought about, it should be brought with a well-financed, capable effort, by people who knew what they were doing in the courts."[87]

The negative consequences of the decision were predictable—and predicted—by the minority dissenters. As a result, the five justices who had forced their opinion on the country rushed to assuage the concerns of dissenting Americans. They declared that religious Americans were still free to speak their mind on the subject of gay marriage, and could invoke divine precepts to make their point. But as Justice Clarence Thomas pointed out, "Religious liberty is about freedom of action in matters of religion generally"—it is not confined to advocacy.[88]

There is little question that the majority justices were much more concerned about the social standing of homosexual individuals than that of people of faith. Six times in the ruling they mentioned "stigma," but in every case it was in reference to gays being stigmatized, not religious persons. Justice Samuel Alito, who possesses a keen sociological

---

[87] *Bill Moyers Journal,* "Theodore Olson and David Boies," aired February 26, 2010, on PBS, https://www.pbs.org/moyers/journal/02262010/profile.html/.

[88] Bill Donohue, "Gay Marriage Ruling Is Ominous," Catholic League, June 26, 2015, https://www.catholicleague.org/gay-marriage-ruling-is-ominous/.

mind, predicted that this decision would be used "to vilify Americas who are unwilling to assent to the new orthodoxy."[89] He was right.

On today's college campuses, it is not the LGBT crowd that is afraid to speak its mind; it is Christian students who hold to traditional moral beliefs. Likewise, in many corporations religious Americans are afraid to speak the truth about marriage, the family, and sexuality.

And it's not over yet. As a result of *Obergefell*, the specter of legalized multi-partner relationships looms: in October 2022, a New York judge ruled that same-sex relationships should not be limited to two people. Here is what happened.

Scott Anderson died in 2021. Markyus O'Neill lived in an apartment with him. Anderson's partner, Robert Romano, lived elsewhere. After Anderson died, O'Neill was forced to give up his rent-controlled apartment because, the landlord said, he was just a roommate. The late Anderson's "life partner of 25 years," the petitioner said, was Romano. The judge, Karen May Bacdayan of the Civil Court of New York, raised the possibility that three men could qualify as a "family-like relationship." In fact, she took issue with *Obergefell* for being too exclusive by limiting its ruling to two men.[90]

---

[89] *Obergefell et al. v. Hodges.*

[90] "New York Judge Paves Way for Recognition of 'Multi-Person Relationships,'" *National Catholic Register*, October 11, 2022, https://www.ncregister.com/cna/new-york-judge-paves-way-for-recognition-of-multi-person-relationships/.

Decades ago, when the issue of gay marriage was first haunting the public square, I debated many of its proponents on radio and TV. I asked them what should be done about a situation where Tom falls in love with Dick and they want to get married, but during their engagement they run into Harry at a party and they both fall in love with him as well. Should we allow Tom, Dick, and Harry to marry? Why leave poor Harry out in the cold? Invariably, my adversaries got mad at me for bringing up such a "preposterous" condition.

It is preposterous no longer.

THE TEN COMMANDMENTS

We were given the Ten Commandments some three thousand years ago. To this day, they are the ultimate rebuke to moral relativism.

Dennis Prager is an observant Jew whose writings on the Ten Commandments are instructive. "Morality, an objective code of right and wrong, does not emanate from human opinion; it emanates from God, and therefore transcends human opinion."[91]

Secularists disagree with Prager. They say they don't need God to tell them that murder is wrong. But according to Prager, this is only partly true:

> I have no doubt that if you're an atheist and you
> say you believe murder is wrong, you believe
> murder is wrong. But, forgive me, you do need

[91] Dennis Prager, *The Ten Commandments: Still the Best Moral Code* (Washington, D.C.: Regnery Publishing, 2015), 3.

God to tell you. We all need God to tell us. You see, even if you figured out that murder is wrong on your own, without God and the Ten Commandments, how do you *know* it's wrong? Not *believe* it's wrong, I mean *know* it's wrong? The fact is that you can't. Because without God, right and wrong are just personal beliefs. Personal opinions. I think shoplifting is okay, you don't. Unless there is a God, all morality is just opinion and belief. And virtually every atheist philosopher has acknowledged this.[92]

While the well-reasoned analysis of natural law can perhaps provide some foundation for morality, even it — ultimately — falls short. And while one does not have to be a believer to recognize that there are some acts that most everyone knows are wrong, unless the role of God is acknowledged, there can be no unassailable certainty.

The moral compass of Western civilization has long been calibrated by the Ten Commandments — and it is the first three commandments particularly that give secularists fits: "I am the Lord thy God, thou shalt not have strange gods before me." "Thou shalt not take the Lord's name in vain." "Thou shalt keep holy the Lord's Day." In a society that embraces radical individualism, the idea of bowing to God is a hard sell.

Secularists are more willing to consider the following seven commandments. But if they thought more about what those commandments imply about human nature,

[92] Ibid., xx.

they might understand why the first three are so important. For example, why did God find it necessary to command us to honor our father and our mother? Why did He command us not to kill? Why did He command us not to commit adultery? Why did He command us not to steal? Why did He command us not to bear false witness against our neighbor? Why did He command us not to covet our neighbor's wife? Why did He command us not to covet our neighbor's goods?

The answer seems obvious: left to our own human appetites, desires, and passions, we incline toward satisfying our self-interest, and that often runs afoul of doing what is morally right. In other words, we must be commanded to treat others morally, lest we do whatever we feel like doing. The Ten Commandments are about others—not ourselves. And they recognize that we do not, by ourselves, have the power to live by truth. We need God.

Aristotle understood that if children do not love their parents and siblings, they would love only themselves. Hence, the necessity of the fourth commandment. The history of man is the history of warfare. It comes naturally to us. This explains why obedience to the fifth commandment is vital. The sex drive is powerful, which makes respect for the sixth and ninth commandments necessary. Revenge and lying do not have to be taught—they are natural to us. But they do need to be curbed, which accounts for the eighth commandment. Envy also comes naturally to us, but it is not an attribute we should encourage—hence the tenth commandment.

But it is astonishing how many secularists find even the last seven commandments stultifying, if not oppressive. Their idea of freedom is narcissistic and therefore antisocial. They fail to appreciate how liberating the Ten Commandments really are—following them allows us to flourish and to reach our potential.

Think of it this way. How free is someone who is a slave to his passions? Are drug addicts free? Are sex maniacs free? Are big-time gamblers free? Are those who eat too much free? Are alcoholics free? Are those who have alienated their family members and their closest friends free? What good is freedom if we can't enjoy it?

In his magnificent encyclical *Veritatis Splendor*, St. John Paul II said the *foundation* of freedom is the Ten Commandments. How so? Because fidelity to them allows us to develop our God-given talents, to tame our worst impulses, and to enjoy the fruits of our freedom. As the saint himself wrote, "Human freedom and God's law are not in opposition; on the contrary, they appeal to one another."[93]

John Paul's central message in this encyclical was "the unbreakable bond between freedom and truth."[94] Regrettably, the secular vision of morality seeks to break that bond.

THE SATANIST CHALLENGE

Thomas Altizer died in 2018, though few people took note. He was the subject of the April 8, 1966, cover of *Time*

---

[93] Bill Donohue, *Why Catholicism Matters* (New York: Image, 2012), 68.

[94] John Paul II, *Veritatis Splendor*, no. 87.

magazine. The black background and the bold red lettering shouted out, "Is God Dead?" (*Time* published this cover in the Easter season, perhaps to poke believers in the eye?)

After Altizer received his Ph.D. in the history of religions from the University of Chicago in 1955, he wanted to become an Episcopal priest. They didn't want him: he flunked the psychiatric exam. In his 2006 memoir, *Living the Death of God*, he finally explained why:

> Shortly before this examination, I was in a turbulent condition. While crossing the Midway I would experience violent tremors in the ground, and I was visited by a deep depression, one that occurred again and again throughout my life, but now with particular intensity. During this period I had perhaps the deepest experience of my life, and one that I believe profoundly affected my vocation as a theologian, and even my theological work. This occurred late at night, while I was in my room. I suddenly awoke and became truly possessed, and experienced an epiphany of Satan which I have never been able to fully deny, an experience in which I could actually feel Satan consuming me, absorbing me into his very being, as though this was the deepest possible initiation and bonding, and the deepest and yet most horrible union.[95]

95 Bill Donohue, "Satan Consumed 'God is Dead' Author," Catholic League, December 3, 2018, https://www.catholicleague.org/satan-consumed-god-is-dead-author/.

A decade after Altizer's satanic possession, he declared the death of God. It's hard not to connect the dots.

That the postmodern assault on truth is the work of the "Father of Lies" may be hard to prove, but Satan must be pleased—and it seems implausible that his hand is entirely absent. Indeed, he is so busy destroying lives that in 2014 Pope Francis formally recognized the International Association of Exorcists; it had been cofounded in 1994 by six priests, including the renowned Fr. Gabriele Amorth. In 2018, news stories noted, "Vatican to Hold Exorcist Training Course after 'Rise in Possessions.'" In 2023, another news story broke, titled "As Exorcisms Demand Continues to Rise, Vatican to Hold Training."

As 2019 came to a close, Dominican Fr. Francois Dermine, an Italian exorcist, observed that "satanism is getting much more aggressive and also diffused." Why? "Secularization leaves a void. Young people do not have anything to satisfy their spiritual and profound needs."[96]

Thomas D. Williams is a brilliant Catholic theologian. It is his belief that the rash of anti-Catholic incidents in recent years—ranging from vandalism to churches being burned to the ground—is tied to satanism. When consecrated Hosts are stolen during the satanic rite called a black mass, there is something going on way beyond mere criminality.[97] After all, it is not the collection basket that is being stolen by satanists.

---

[96] Thomas D. Williams, *The Coming Christian Persecution: Why Things Are Getting Worse and What You Can Do about It* (Manchester, NH: Crisis, 2023), 155.

[97] Ibid., 156–157.

Satanic-inspired crimes are no ordinary crimes. Jimmy Savile was a famous pedophile in England who spent his adult life working for the BBC. Before he died in 2011, he was believed to be responsible for abusing at least 450 males and females, aged eight to forty-seven. As one news story reported, he "beat and raped a 12-year-old girl during a secret satanic ritual in a hospital" in 1992. During the rape, he and his cohorts, also pedophiles, chanted, "Hail Satan" in a candle-lit room. Five years later, he abused another girl during a black mass ceremony. She, too, heard Latin chanting and witnessed a group of men wearing satanist regalia.[98]

Many similar stories could be told, but none more well-known than the violent deeds of cult leader Charles Manson. He told the media, "I am the devil." The reporters failed to follow up.

There is another Manson, Marilyn, who commands our attention. He was best known for his music that glorifies evil. A member of the Church of Satan, he publicly identified as Lucifer. While performing, he ripped up Bibles and sold T-shirts that read "Kill Your Parents." The names of his songs show his mindset: "GodEatGod," "Cruci-Fiction in Space," "President Dead," "In the Shadow of the Valley of Death," "The Death Song," "The Lamb of God," and "Count to Six and Die." On the cover of his album *Holy Wood* was a depiction of a baby nailed to a cross.

[98] Bill Donohue, "Satanism Linked to Serial Crimes," Catholic League, January 15, 2013, https://www.catholicleague.org/satanism-linked-to-serial-crimes/.

Nothing attracts the attention of satanists as much as abortion. In 2020, in Bellingham, Washington, pro-life students prayed outside a Planned Parenthood abortion mill, and for this "crime" they were subjected to obscenities and harassment. A man masturbated in his car in front of students, a woman flashed them, and a man threw a glass vial at them. Another woman yelled at them, "We don't need your prayers. Hail Satan!"[99]

Detroit is home to the Satanic Temple, the most rabid pro-abortion satanist organization in the nation. It likes to promote what it calls the "Abortion Ritual," which is designed to "cast off unwanted feelings" associated with taking the life of an unborn child. It involves reciting the third tenet of the Satanic Temple: "One's body is inviolable, subject to one's own will alone."

The mission statement of the Satanic Temple says it "offers legal protection against laws that unscientifically restrict women's reproductive autonomy." So sacred is abortion to these satanists that they have a "Religious Rights Reproductive Rights Campaign." It advocates on behalf of the so-called religious rights of satanists to campaign for abortion.

The Satanic Temple has a list of legal restrictions it finds objectionable: they range from ultrasound tests that allow the mother to hear the heartbeat of her baby to mandatory waiting periods. They also seek to undermine crisis pregnancy centers. So zealous are the satanists in their quest for

[99] Bill Donohue, "Satan Enters Abortion Politics," Catholic League, March 11, 2020, https://www.catholicleague.org/satan-enters-abortion-politics/.

abortion rights that they oppose burial rights for the remains of children who have been aborted.

In 2018, I decided to engage the Satanic Temple on this issue. Here is the email exchange.

> Q: "I'm curious. Why is abortion such a big issue for satanists?"
>
> A: "It isn't abortion per se, it is personal freedom."
>
> Q: "But if the personal freedom of a woman to have an abortion results in the wholesale denial of personal freedom for her baby, how is that a victory for liberty?"
>
> A: "Because it isn't a baby."[100]

The "Father of Lies" has always led the war on Christianity—and the war on the innocent. While most of those who support abortion rights are not satanists, and may even object to what they say and do, when the very concept of truth is doubted or denied, it is a short walk to perdition.

The secular vision of man and society is morally empty. It is responsible for our cultural meltdown and for the social debris it has left in its wake. We know the right remedy is a return to our religious roots. We must pray more people will come to know the truth.

---

[100] Bill Donohue, "Satanists Love Abortion," Catholic League, November 16, 2018, https://www.catholicleague.org/satanists-love-abortion/.

PART II

SEXUAL SABOTAGE

CHAPTER 3

LIBERTINISM

THE PRICE OF PAGANISM

TODAY'S SECULAR VISION OF liberty is very much in the pagan tradition, discarding truth as a chimera and seeing morality as a repressive code of conduct. The religious vision—and particularly the Christian vision—maintains that without a moral consensus, grounded in eternal truths, the social order crumbles. The two visions could not be further apart. Alas, the Western world has moved decisively away from the religious model, and is attempting to implement a radical individualism that springs from the secular vision of morality.

Max Boot is a well-known neoconservative writer. He is also an atheist. He maintains that the secular vision of morality is preferable to the religious one, arguing that "Rome fell after it converted to Christianity."[101] Not so fast. The suggestion that Christianity caused the decline of Rome is

---

[101] Max Boot, "Yes, We Are Less Religious. We're Also Better Off," *Washington Post*, February 20, 2020, A19.

historically without merit. In fact, Boot's anti-Christian hypothesis was debunked as early as the fifth century by none other than St. Augustine.

Augustine spent thirteen years writing his famous book *The City of God*. In this fifteen-hundred-page work, he thoroughly refutes the idea that Christianity brought about the decline of Rome. It was not Christianity that caused Rome to collapse, he says. Rather, it was the moral decadency ingrained in paganism that was responsible. Augustine drew on Roman historians Livy and Sallust, who had described how paganism had failed, and he illustrated how the virtues of Christianity, rather than undermining the state, in fact buttressed good citizenship.

But Augustine was really echoing wisdom found in the Bible, particularly with respect to personal freedom and what it truly means to be free. In Galatians we read, "For freedom Christ set us free; so stand firm and do not submit again to the yoke of slavery" (5:1). And again, "For you were called for freedom, brothers. But do not use this freedom as an opportunity for the flesh; rather, serve one another through love" (5:13). The Catholic understanding of freedom and morality is not one of license, or libertinism. It is not a free-for-all where each individual makes up his own moral code. It is based on individual responsibilities to others and on fidelity to the truth as written in the Scriptures.

These biblical exhortations were rejected by the pagans in Rome, and they are rejected by today's pagans as well. For example, sexual morality in the Roman Empire was permissive. Homosexual relationships were common (though same-sex marriage was not given legal sanction). Man-boy pedophilia was widely approved and practiced; there was nothing shameful about older men pursuing young boys. It was also considered morally acceptable for men to have sex with slaves and prostitutes. In fact, prostitution was regarded as proper for a man, an acceptable way for him to "sow his oats"—and was even acceptable for a husband while married; it was not considered adultery. By contrast, women were expected to be virgins before marriage, and loyal wives afterwards.

The Christian vision of sexuality could not have been more different. Homosexuality was taboo, as was man-boy sex. Men were expected to be as chaste as women. Prostitution was not condoned. Sexual activity was confined to a man and a woman in the institution of marriage. These norms finally became prevalent under the reign of Justinian (527–565). This was the Christian sexual revolution. Among other things, it was a huge step forward for women.

Thomas Paprocki, bishop of the Diocese of Springfield, Illinois, understands the importance of the Christian sexual revolution. In an interview with Raymond Arroyo, he said,

> It was actually Christianity that brought about a sexual revolution in the first century because many of the things that are being proposed today in terms of free expressions of sexuality—that was very common in the pagan Roman Empire—and Christians came along and said, "No, we're not going to live that way. Men don't share their wives with other people." And so they

started living in a way that was faithful between a man and a wife and was excluding sexual relationships outside of marriage. That was the first sexual revolution. And it seems to me there are people who want to disregard what the practice of Christianity has been for the past two thousand years and go back to the practices of the ancient Roman Empire.[102]

What Bishop Paprocki said is undeniably true. There is no end to the number of people, many of whom are found in elite institutions, who promote a libertine conception of sexuality. Their idea of liberty begins and ends with the individual, and has little to do with marriage, family, or the social order. It is a prescription for disorder, and it undermines freedom, properly understood. The Catholic understanding of freedom is the right to do what we ought to do; it is not the freedom to do whatever we want to do.

Edmund Burke, the father of conservatism, held that without wisdom and virtue, liberty "is the greatest of all possible evils; for it is folly, vice and madness without tuition or restraint."[103] Liberty and restraint are not polar opposite. They go hand in hand. Even Sigmund Freud understood that restraint was the price we pay for civilization, even if it causes "discontent." Yet without putting a lid on our libido, we are playing with fire. A riot of the id,

[102] Bishop Thomas Paprocki, interview by Raymond Arroyo, *The World Over*, aired March 2, 2023, on EWTN.
[103] Brad Lowell Stone, *Robert Nisbet* (Wilmington, DE: ISI Books, 2002), 65.

the pleasure principle, causes much more than discontent — it produces social decomposition.

WEIMAR GERMANY

Hitler's rise to power was caused by many factors. But often overlooked are the cultural forces that contributed to his ascendency. From 1871 to 1914, Germany was a very stable society. Life was routine: marriages, families, school, work, and religion were a source of unity and contentment. Then came World War I.

The period in Germany from the end of World War I to the beginning of Nazi Germany, 1918–1933, is known as the Weimar Republic. It was a time of total disarray. Hitler successfully exploited the alienation and the discontent that the German people felt after losing the war and being humiliated by the draconian provisions of the Versailles Treaty. By strangling Germany with enormous reparations, the victors pummeled the vanquished into submission and created a strong sense of resentment.

Germany lost the war because it was militarily and economically exhausted — and because of the intervention of the United States. But this was not what most Germans believed. They believed that some of their own people had turned on their war effort, saying it felt like a "stab in the back." For example, the Nazis said that Germany was betrayed in 1917 by pacifists who worked to force the end of the war. Moreover, members of the Social Democratic Party called on those building armaments to walk off the job, and a munitions strike created a psychological crisis for frontline soldiers. In the military, sailors engaged in mutiny and soldiers deserted. In November 1918, rioters attacked officers returning from the war and beat them in the streets.

Then, after the war, the economy tanked. Inflation was so bad that restaurants would change the price of meals while diners were eating. Then came the Great Depression. Then unemployment.

But in addition to these grueling political and economic challenges, Germany witnessed a moral collapse. This collapse catalyzed Hitler's monstrous rise to power.

Libertinism ruled the day. Prostitution, pornography, and homosexuality were rampant. The moral bar dropped so low that people had sex in public. One reason for this decadence was demographic: so many men had been killed or severely injured in the war that it created a sex ratio imbalance — millions more women than men. The social seed for what was dubbed "the new woman" had been planted. But the fruit of the tree wasn't female empowerment; it was a spike in public nudity, homosexuality, hedonism, and street prostitution. The cabaret society drew tourists; but it also drew a criminal element as the sex tourism industry took off.

Homosexual and lesbian bars exploded in German cities. In Berlin there were scores of gay and lesbian bars. On-stage nudity was commonplace, and prostitution was legalized in 1927. Lawmakers supported these efforts, arguing that the German people had suffered enough and needed opportunities to let off steam.

Sexologists played a major role in promoting the moral debasement of Germany. A Dutch gynecologist, Theodoor

Hendrik van de Velde, was one of the most prominent. His sex manual, *Ideal Marriage*, was widely read in Germany. The key to "enduring happiness" in marriage lay in ongoing sexual pleasure. He went to great lengths specifying how women could experience a new sex life, and graphically informed men of what they needed to do to accomplish this end.

Another sexologist who outdid even Velde was a young German doctor named Magnus Hirschfeld. He went beyond Velde by embracing homosexuality, and he used his authority to promote a more satisfying social and legal environment for homosexuals.

What made him really unusual was his conviction that there were persons who did not fit the categories of heterosexual or homosexual. He argued there was a "third sex" that existed naturally. These "sexual intermediaries" were bisexuals and transvestites. In doing so, he laid the intellectual groundwork for transgenderism and opened the door to what are now called gender fluid and non-binary persons. In fact, Hirschfeld's Institute for Sexual Research in Berlin is credited with opening the world's first transgender clinic.[104]

To die-hard secularists, both then and today, Weimar Germany was a sexual paradise, a place where sexual expression was not condemned but rather prized. Their myopia is astounding. The sexual paradise produced rampant sexual diseases, especially syphilis. Prostitution helped undermine

[104] Brandy Schillace, "The Forgotten History of the World's First Trans Clinic," *Scientific American*, May 10, 2021, https://www.scientificamerican.com/article/the-forgotten-history-of-the-worlds-first-trans-clinic/.

marriages, which were already strained by economic forces. If an epidemic of venereal diseases, broken marriages, and abortions is considered progress, it is hard to know what would convince secularists of the intellectual and moral shallowness of their views.

To their credit, Catholic and Protestant leaders reacted strongly to Weimar decadence. Christian leaders rallied the faithful to make strong families their priority. They called for a reinvigoration of Christian morality at every level of society.

But they were not alone. Even artists were able to see the decadence of the period. More than anyone, George Grosz offered the most authoritative artistic telling of what happened. He did not seek to understand what had happened to Germany during the Weimar Republic; his forte was in accurately portraying what happened. He painted what he saw, which was "the moral collapse of Germany."[105] Because he was not bound to any cause or organization, historians consider his work to be a faithful representation of the moral degradation that occurred during the Weimar period.

If the moral collapse of Germany was confined to issues of marriage and the family alone, many secularists would conclude that it is not sufficient to question the benefits of sexual liberation. They are wrong in that assessment. There is a direct line between the moral collapse of Weimar Germany and the ascendancy of Hitler. They need to connect the dots.

[105] Ted Loos, "Books in Brief: Nonfiction; He Drew Them As He Saw Them," *New York Times*, August 24, 1997, Section 7, p. 18, Column 2, Book Review Desk.

Societies, like individuals, can be healthy or they can be sick. When individuals get sick, it is because they have contracted an illness, sometimes brought about by their own doing—overeating, excessive drinking, taking drugs, neglecting sleep, overwork. The same is true of society. When there is a sense of community and civility, society is healthy and it functions well. When the family, religious institutions, and voluntary associations are humming along, that's a sign of social health. But when disequilibrium rules, when things get out of whack, trouble follows.

Hitler exploited the moral disorder by promising to repair it. He presented himself as a messiah called by fate to restore Germany to its rightful prominence on the world stage. He believed he represented the German national will—the *Volk*—and shouted that he was the man who would give Germans a sense of community once again. His Storm Troopers were portrayed as "purifiers" who would bring about a secular millennium, a "Third Reich."

In other words, Nazism was proclaimed as a utopian vision, made necessary and possible because of the moral collapse of Germany.

When the moral order collapses, society becomes atomized and descends to a level of raw individualism. But people really want order and a sense of belonging. In other words, by pushing an agenda of radical individualism, especially with regards to sexuality, the German secularists created the kind of disequilibrium that Hitler said he would rectify. His Nazi ideal of *Volksgemeinschaft* was a state where a strong sense of community—of oneness—once again prevailed; it became the solution to a moral problem.

If there is one lesson we should learn from this, it is that extremes invite extremes: pushing individual liberty to extremes creates social chaos, which in turn cries out for an extremist response. Wise people will settle for a measure of freedom, a moderate course that constrains base appetites.

As always, when social and cultural disorder occurs, we don't have to look far to find the intellectual hand at work. Duke University professor Claudia Koonz wrote a book, *The Nazi Conscience*, in which she showed how Hitler actually downplayed his anti-Semitism when he ascended to power so as to maintain an air of respectability. Surprisingly, she also asserts that the Germans, before Hitler's rise, were the least anti-Semitic people in Europe. So what made them change? She cites the role of public intellectuals and the scientific community. They worked alongside the Nazi propagandists to shape a new culture. Together, they "reeducated" the German people and taught them to hate Jews.[106]

The "reeducation" could not have proceeded unless the German people were culturally ripe for the pickings—and it succeeded because Germany was in a state of anomie, or normlessness, in which deciding right from wrong was totally confusing.

I once had an occasion to show my college students how libertinism generates the normlessness that allows for some

[106] Jack Fischel, "Nazi Morals," review of *The Nazi Conscience* by Claudia Koonz, *The Weekly Standard*, January 12, 2004, 30–31.

horrible things to happen. I was discussing the detrimental effects of hard-core pornography, and I noticed two students smirking. I asked them to consider why ordinary Germans allowed for the extermination of Jews under the Nazis. I explained that Albert Speer, one of Hitler's top officials, said he never hated Jews, he just depersonalized them. I then asked them what they thought were the effects on the psyche of those who watch "snuff films" over and over again—movies that show horrifying images like trucks running over the heads of women, with their brains scattered about the road. Once we depersonalize, horrible things can happen. They got the point.

In the end, the defeat in World War I, the humiliation of the Treaty of Versailles, the skyrocketing inflation, the Great Depression, and the moral collapse—these are the factors that prepared the social soil Hitler capitalized on, promising rejuvenation. What he delivered was genocide. This is consistent with research done on the causes of genocidal movements, which typically depend on a state of anomie.

Anomie is what characterizes American society today. This does not necessarily mean that we are sowing totalitarianism. But it does mean that the weeds of our increasingly libertine culture are strangling our sense of community, and choking the families that are struggling to survive.

INTELLECTUALS VS. THE FAMILY

Most people have little in common with radical intellectuals. Most people go to school, or work, or enjoy leisure time with their family. Most people do not spend their lives thinking of ways to transform society. Most people do not occupy positions of power, or even influence those who hold power. But left-wing intellectuals do. And they look to the state, the supreme political organ in society, to implement their plans to restructure society.

Standing in the way of their plans are the bedrock social institutions that comprise civil society, most especially the family and the church. That is why intellectuals seek to disable them.

Left-wing intellectuals look to Marx as their mentor. He also hated the family and the church. Ironically, he looked to the urban working class, the proletariat, to usher in socialism and eventually Communism. But the working class, despite its economic circumstances, usually has little interest in promoting revolution. The working class is typically comprised of normal people who want a normal life. This was understood by the "cultural Marxists." They realized that the best way to create a revolution in capitalist societies was to bring about a cultural transformation, not an economic one.

Marxists who favored a cultural revolution took root in Germany in the late 1920s and early 1930s, at the end of the Weimar Republic. They are known as the Frankfurt School. In the mid-1930s, major figures in the movement moved to New York City and took up posts at Columbia University. They brought their toxic blend of Freud and Marx with them.

Most of these intellectuals lived a libertine existence, and they sought to make their lifestyle the norm for everyone else. Their hatred of the family centered on the father who, according to them, had too much power. Patriarchy, the family norm throughout the ages (and a norm overwhelmingly supported by women), was branded by the cultural Marxists as "authoritarian" because it inhibited their idea of liberty. Hierarchy, they declared, was by its very nature oppressive—and hierarchy begins with the family and the authority exercised by the father.

One of the most famous members of the Frankfurt School was Theodor Adorno. He wrote *The Authoritarian Personality*, a book that sought to portray the father as the source of oppression. Most fathers, he reasoned, held to traditional norms and values, and were committed to family and religion. That's why their authority had to be undermined. Who better to do the job than teachers and instructors indoctrinated by Frankfurt School propaganda? If this sounds familiar, it should. It's the face of "progressivism" today.

How else to destroy the family? The Hungarian cultural Marxist Georg Lukács recommended fostering a culture of libertinism. But in order to allow radical ideas of sexuality to take root, the Judeo-Christian sexual ethic of restraint had to be attacked. Again, the schools provided a vehicle. To be explicit, he pushed for a sex education curriculum. He did not mean teaching about the birds and the bees; he meant a course of study where sexual expression without limits was taught in the schools. Neither parents nor religious authorities, he held, should be allowed to thwart this program.

Lukács explicitly wanted to teach children to be sexual adventurers—and he actually succeeded for a while: in 1919, he was the culture and education commissar of Hungary. His biographer explained his pedagogy: "Special lectures were organized in schools and literature printed and distributed to 'instruct' children about free love, about the nature of sexual intercourse, about the archaic nature of bourgeois family codes, about the outdatedness of monogamy, and the irrelevance of religion, which deprives man of all pleasure. Children urged thus to reject and deride parental authority and the authority of the church, and to ignore precepts of morality."[107]

That's about as good a lesson plan for destroying the family and fostering libertinism as anyone could devise.

Wilhelm Reich was perhaps the most sexually crazed member of the Frankfurt School. His psychoanalytic writings savaged Catholic teachings on sexuality. Influenced by Freud—who said the "real enemy" was the Catholic Church—Reich is known as the "Father of the Sexual Revolution." He was not content to live a libertine lifestyle. Like Lukács, he wanted to get to the kids and indoctrinate them with his radical sexual ideas. He wanted children to abandon their Catholicism and embrace Communism. But he believed that there could be no political revolution without first witnessing a sexual revolution.

Freud saw sexual restraint as the unfortunate price we pay for civilization. But Reich refused to pay the price—and his life did not have a happy ending. He was convicted of fraud and died in prison.

More than any other of the Frankfurt School cultural Marxists, it was Herbert Marcuse who really made his name in the United States. Like his colleagues, he hated the family

---

[107] Mike Gonzalez, "Socialism and Family," Heritage Foundation, March 1, 2022, https://www.heritage.org/node/24968989/.

and glorified libertinism. American students who identified with the "New Left" in the 1960s looked at him as their intellectual godfather. He saw oppression everywhere, and he focused his attention on the need to liberate men and women from the yoke of religious oppression. He envisioned the emergence of a "new person," a creature who would no longer take his cues from "established society." He imagined a utopian world where war and aggression would cease to exist.

Marcuse advocated "polymorphous perversity," a condition where everyone enjoys as many sexual experiences as possible, with as many people as possible. Nothing was taboo—his idea of liberty was a sexual free-for-all. He neglected to tell his followers about the joys of sexually transmitted diseases. No doubt some of them made an early trip to their grave. But such is the price of libertinism.

I had a chance to discuss how libertinism kills when I participated in the last *Firing Line* team debate that William F. Buckley Jr. televised in 1998 at Bard College. The topic of the debate was the ACLU. The top two ACLU officials were joined by two left-wing activists; two other conservatives joined Buckley and me on the other team.

When I was asked by Nadine Strossen, president of the ACLU, why I opposed sex education, the left-wing student audience laughed. I answered, "I am not opposed to it. I take a much more Catholic understanding of sex education perhaps, which emphasizes restraint. More people would be alive today if they followed the Catholic Church's teaching." After some back and forth, I concluded my remarks by saying to the smirking students that if more people practiced restraint, they would "not go to as many funerals."[108] There was no laughter. Just dead silence.

The debased vision of morality is not confined to the classroom. It is celebrated today by the cultural Marxists who comprise Black Lives Matter. How so? They have said that it is their goal to destroy the nuclear family. The black family is in enough trouble, for all kinds of reasons, without its purported allies wanting to finish it off. The Ku Klux Klan could not develop a more devious and pernicious formula for attacking the black community.

Canadian historian William D. Gairdner writes that "totalitarian movements always seek to weaken family institutions so that men, women, and children will become equally subordinate to the State."[109] That is the goal of the self-professed Marxists who founded Black Lives Matter. It is the expressed goal of the Left, in general. These ideologues are driven by the pursuit of power and control over the minds and bodies of everyone. They preach liberty, but their goal is domination by the state.

CELEBRATING PERVERSIONS

Normal people regard people with perversions as sick and in need of help. Many left-wing intellectuals—who often do not want to be regarded as normal, and indeed reject the idea

[108] "A Firing Line Debate: Resolved: That the ACLU Is Full Of Baloney," *Firing Line*, May 4, 1998, transcript FLS no. 205/ PBS no. 205, 39.
[109] William D. Gairdner, *The Book of Absolutes: A Critique of Relativism and a Defense of Universals* (Montreal: McGill-Queen's University Press, 2008), 278.

of normalcy—not only disagree that perverts are abnormal, but they want to celebrate them.

The word *sadism* is derived from the name of the Marquis de Sade, the late-eighteenth-century French writer. He was a pervert extraordinaire who urged everyone to model themselves on his ways. No form of pornography could satisfy him; his tastes were blunted by excess. Sexual experimentation, he said, should have no bounds.

Not surprisingly, de Sade hated the Catholic Church. He spent his days preaching the necessity of destroying the Church, and his nights destroying himself. He delighted in depicting the clergy as perverts, bishops having anal sex with girls. His hatred of Catholicism was so pathological that it enticed him to defile the Mass. He even paid a prostitute to trample on a crucifix. They finally locked him away in an asylum. Today his ilk would condemn the decision to send him away, rather than criticize the words and deeds that got him committed.

Those who think that only perverts like de Sade would profess such diabolical ideas and practices are quite mistaken. Byron and Shelley were nineteenth-century English poets who commanded the respect of elite society. They also waxed eloquent on the merits of incest. Freud went even further: he called the taboo against incest "perhaps the most drastic mutilation which man's erotic life has in all time experienced."[110]

---

[110] Sigmund Freud, *Civilization and Its Discontents* (New York: Norton, 1961), 51.

It's not just male writers who have been drawn to defend indefensible sexual acts. In the United States, feminist Shulamith Firestone took a page from Freud and advocated the abolition of the incest taboo. Though she was mentally ill, she commanded quite an audience. Only when the family and the incest taboo are destroyed, she said, would sexuality "be released from its straightjacket to eroticize our whole culture, changing its very definition."[111] Like Wilhelm Reich, she posited a direct link between a sexual revolution and a political revolution. In fact, she blamed the failure of the Russian Revolution on the failure to "eliminate the family and sexual repression."[112]

More recently, another radical feminist, Judith Butler, has argued that we need to get rid of the incest taboo because incest is not necessarily a traumatic act; what is traumatic is the stigmatization itself. She is another intellectual who ties political revolution to sexual revolution. She argues for the creation of a coalition of activists who are opposed to racism, economic injustice, and colonialism, saying it is necessary to achieve "queer politics." She also promotes anarchy.

Anne Hendershott is a crackerjack Catholic sociologist who understands the mindset of these people. Her analysis of the influential French philosopher Michel Foucault (about whom much more will be said below) is spot-on: "According to Foucault, things like madness, murder, incest, prostitution, homosexuality, illegal drug use and robbery

[111] Shulamith Firestone, *The Dialectic of Sex* (New York: Bantam Books, 1971), 60.
[112] Ibid., 212.

were not 'deviance'; they were 'categories of censure' which gradually created, developed or re-formed in the course of establishing and mapping out new systems and territories of domination."[113] Got that? Predictably, Foucault also considered laws forbidding man-boy sex to be cruel, and he advocated for the abolition of all laws that sanctioned sexual conduct, including rape.

Perhaps no one played a more significant role sexualizing American society than Alfred Kinsey. He was a zoologist-turned-sexologist. His research and writings on male and female sexuality, published after World War II, were the topic of discussion in living rooms across the nation, as well as in classrooms. Most knew him as simply a scientist who offered new insights into the way men, and especially women, could enjoy a more robust sex life. They did not know that he was a scientific fraud, a pervert, a voyeur, an exhibitionist, a masochist, a gay-bar-hopping homosexual (even though he was married), and a child abuser. Oh, yes, he also had sex with animals.

Anthropologist Margaret Mead, whose writings on sexuality, as well as her own sexual practices, were anything but conventional, said that in Kinsey's view there was no moral difference between a man having sex with a woman or a sheep. But author Judith Reisman provides actual information about Kinsey that is even more shocking.

Reisman spent a good part of her life investigating Kinsey's work. In his research, he used kids as guinea pigs. In

[113] Anne Hendershott, *The Politics of Deviance* (San Francisco: Encounter Books, 2002), 5.

fact, he sexually abused over three hundred children: he instructed his "researchers" to sexually stimulate infants as young as two months old to try to give them orgasms. In some cases, the children were stimulated nonstop for over twenty-four hours. At least one of these "researchers" was a pedophile who masturbated and penetrated children. Another one of his researchers, known as "Mr. X," sexually abused six hundred boys and two hundred girls—he kept a log of his achievements. He also had sex with seventeen blood relatives, including his own grandmother.[114]

It goes without saying that Kinsey hated Christianity. He spent his entire adult life in rebellion against his "strict" Protestant parents. But he saved his most hateful comments for Catholicism, and saw the Church as the pinnacle of repression.

Normal people don't act this way. Sexual freaks and child abusers do. We will never know whether Kinsey's hatred for the Catholic Church arose from the guilt that he must have felt from his behavior, or from his anger at the Church's sexual ethics. But his obsession with Catholicism cannot be doubted. Strangely, he blamed Christianity, not libertinism, for the breakdown of the modern family. It apparently never occurred to him that his own work played an important role in the collapse of the family.

In a review of the 2004 movie *Kinsey*, *New York Times* critic Caleb Crain wrote that "Kinsey had had affairs with men, encouraged open marriages among his staff,

---

[114] Bill Donohue, *Secular Sabotage: How Liberals Are Destroying Religion and Culture in America* (New York: FaithWords, 2009), 40.

stimulated himself with urethral insertion and ropes, and filmed sex in his attic." He said that "the most controversial scene in the movie is Kinsey's infamous meeting with a sexual omnivore, whose history of sexual encounters with men, women, boys, girls, animals and family members took 17 hours to record."[115]

No wonder modern-day pedophiles are so fond of Kinsey. NAMBLA, the North American Man/Boy Love Association, remembers him on their website. Indeed, it is fitting that they acknowledge him, given what Kinsey had to say in his book *Sexual Behavior in the Human Female*: "When children are constantly warned by parents and teachers against contacts with adults, and when they receive no explanation of the exact nature of the contacts, they are ready to become hysterical as soon as any older person approaches, or stops and speaks to them in the street, *or fondles them*, or proposes to do something for them, even though the adult may have had no sexual objective in mind."[116]

In other words, men who fondle children are not the problem—those who object to such fondling are, which explains why Kinsey wrote, "The current hysteria over sex offenders may very well have serious effects on the ability of many of these children to work out sexual adjustments some years later."[117] In his twisted mind, Kinsey thought that if kids are not open to being sexually aroused by adults, their

[115] Bill Donohue, "Indiana Univ. Honors a Pervert," Catholic League, September 14, 2002, https://www.catholicleague.org/indiana-univ-honors-a-pervert/.

[116] Ibid. My emphasis.

[117] Ibid.

resistance—not the molesting act—might lead to sexual dysfunction later in life.

School officials at Indiana University (home to the Kinsey Institute where he worked) know about his perversions. But they still love him. In 2022, they honored him by erecting a large bronze sculpture of him on the Bloomington campus to mark the seventy-fifth anniversary of the institute. Kinsey may be the only serial predator and child abuser ever to be intentionally celebrated on a college campus.

Given its view of Kinsey, perhaps it is not surprising that Indiana University hosts an annual "sex fest" on campus. It typically features "kink" and sex toys, as well as demonstrations on how to engage in bondage, dominance, submission, and masochism (BDSM). In 2020, it also showed a video depicting a man publicly paddling a woman tied to a St. Andrew's cross in a dorm room. Bear in mind, this is a state school, which means taxpayers—most of whom are Christian—are paying for this "education."

But Ivy League schools are also promoting libertinism. In 2022, Princeton University started offering classes on BDSM, as well as fetishism. Students could enroll, for credit, in courses such as "Black + Queer in Leather: Black Leather/ BDSM Material Culture" and "Anthropology of Religion: Fetishism and Decolonization." What line of work such classes prepare students to perform is unclear.

Kinsey may have been the king of sexual freaks in the United States, but his appetite for exploiting children is shared by many left-wing intellectuals, particularly French intellectuals: in 1977, a number of the most prominent signed a petition seeking to throw out all the laws on sex between adults and minors. Among them were Jacques Derrida, Louis Althusser, Jean-Paul Sartre, Simone de Beauvoir, André Glucksmann, and Roland Barthes. Perhaps the most radical intellectual to sign the petition was Michel Foucault. He deserves his own special treatment.

FOUCAULT

"At the time of his death on June 25, 1984, at the age of fifty-seven, Michel Foucault was perhaps the single most famous intellectual in the world. His books, essays, and interviews had been translated into sixteen languages. Social critics treated his work as a touchstone."[118] This is an accurate description of him, written by his biographer, James Miller. Miller left out that Foucault was also one of the most depraved men ever to walk the face of the earth.

Before examining his contribution to libertinism, let's learn a little more about the man himself.

Like so many male atheist intellectuals, Foucault had what Catholic psychologist Paul Vitz calls a "defective father syndrome."[119] The retired New York University professor studied the biographies of many atheist intellectuals, looking for a common thread. He discovered that the most prominent intellectuals tended to have had serious problems, of one kind or another, with their fathers. They

---

[118] James Miller, *The Passion of Michel Foucault* (New York: Anchor Books, 1993), 13.

[119] Bill Donohue, *Why Catholicism Matters* (New York: Image, 2012), xviii.

also had an animus toward authority and a strong penchant for individualism, which helps explain why they refuse to answer to anyone. It also explains their problem with God, the ultimate authority.

What Vitz revealed applies perfectly to Foucault. He both detested his father and wanted "very much to be loved."[120] Prone to self-destructive acts, he joked about hanging himself and several times attempted suicide, including by slashing his wrists. Obsessed with death, Foucault also reminded some people of the Marquis de Sade, one of his heroes. He defended "everyone's right to kill himself," calling suicide "the simplest of pleasures." He offered specific advice on how to finish the job.[121]

Another one of Foucault's obsessions was power. In many respects, he was a French version of Nietzsche, the German nihilist. According to the literary critic Edmund Wilson, "Michel Foucault was a man deeply attracted to power in its most totalitarian form, politically and sexually."[122]

Foucault's attraction to power had a destructive component to it: he wanted the "demolition of modern society as a cohesive, integrated totality."[123] Above all else he sought to free society of cultural and political conservatism, though he had little to say about what he envisioned after society disintegrated.

[120] Miller, *The Passion of Michel Foucault*, 330.
[121] Ibid., 54–55.
[122] Ibid., 281.
[123] Ibid., 199.

Like so many left-wing intellectuals, Foucault was enthralled with violence. He took great delight when radical students rioted in Paris in 1968, bragging that "the system is being shattered."[124] The next year he "gleefully" threw rocks at the police but, as Miller says, was "careful not to dirty his beautiful black velour suit."[125] Authority of every kind had to be defeated, save for the authority he craved.

Foucault was the quintessential moral relativist. He believed that there was no fundamental difference between democracies and totalitarian states. Oppression existed everywhere, and it was his job to educate his followers so they could eradicate it. For three years, in the 1950s, he joined the Communist Party; while he abandoned it rather quickly, he never moderated his views. If anything, his extremism only got worse. He supported genocidal monsters like Mao Zedong and the Ayatollah Khomeini—it made no difference if they were on the left or the right. What mattered was the exhibition of raw power.

But it was Foucault's commitment to sexual liberation that secured his place as a champion of libertinism. There was not a sexually debased act that he did not countenance, or for that matter practice. But in the course of trying to destroy society, he wound up destroying himself. Noam Chomsky is one of America's most noted left-wing intellectuals. When he

[124] Ibid., 198.
[125] Roger Kimball, "The Perversions of M. Foucault," *New Criterion*, March 1993, https://newcriterion.com/print/article/4714/.

says of Foucault, "I'd never met anyone who was so amoral," that's saying something.[126]

For Foucault, there were no boundaries; if we are going to change the world, he said, we must first "change our selves, our bodies, our souls." The future society was one in which we could bask in drugs and sex.

Foucault anticipated what it would be like to live a life of libertinism. He took LSD and engaged in sadomasochistic acts. Regarding the latter, he said, "I think that S/M is … the real creation of new possibilities of pleasure." Similarly, he believed that drugs "can produce very intense pleasure."[127] It was always about pleasure. It was never about joy or happiness.

To appreciate how depraved Foucault was, consider the kinds of behaviors he promoted and practiced. Among the experiences that gave him pleasure were "gagging, piercing, cutting, electric-shocking, stretching on racks, imprisoning, branding." He acquired a slew of leather clothes, as well as "clamps, handcuffs, hoods, gags, whips, paddles, and other 'sex toys.'"[128] Normal people see such behaviors as sick. But many of Foucault's colleagues and followers found them ecstatic.

As Foucault aptly put it, "Sex is worth dying for."[129] But the people he had sex with made him a total pervert. "To die for the love of boys. What could be more beautiful?"[130] Rape?

[126] Miller, *The Passion of Michel Foucault*, 201.
[127] Ibid., 263.
[128] Kimball, "The Perversions of M. Foucault."
[129] Miller, *The Passion of Michel Foucault*, 243.
[130] Ibid., 350.

He delighted in it, especially child rape. A philosopher he befriended, Guy Sorman, said that when the "great intellectual" was in Tunis, he witnessed "young children running after Foucault asking him for the money he offered other children before raping them." The boys were eight, nine, or ten years of age. He raped them in a cemetery atop gravestones. As Sorman said, "The question of consent wasn't even raised."[131]

Foucault treated his body like a human garbage can. When he visited the United States, he went to San Francisco and spent his time in gay bars, clubs, and bathhouses, bragging about all the orgies he experienced. Miller notes that he was entranced by the gay scene there, and how they "facilitated an exuberant outpouring of experimentation with new forms of self-expression, new styles of libertinism, new blends of drugs and sex, new—and sometimes prodigiously imaginative—combinations of 'bodies and pleasures.'"[132]

Ever the postmodernist, Foucault believed there was no such thing as truth and that everything in life was a social construct. As it turned out, it was this transparently stupid notion—a notion so many intellectuals say they believe—that ultimately killed him. AIDS was first diagnosed in 1981. He didn't believe in it and said the disease was nothing more than puritanical hysteria.[133] In the end, he died of a disease that he insisted was just another social construct. But social constructs don't kill. Libertinism does.

---

[131] Douglas Murray, *The War on the West* (New York: Broadside Books, 2022), 181–182.

[132] Miller, *The Passion of Michel Foucault*, 253.

[133] Ibid., 345.

TARGETING THE KIDS

Those who view liberty as license may not all wind up dead like Foucault. But their chances of winding up with out-of-wedlock pregnancies and sexually transmitted diseases are quite good. Many Hollywood celebrities, many of those who run the movie studios, and many academics have been promoting a corrupt idea of liberty for decades—and their lives are a mess as a result. But perhaps the greatest danger these elites pose to others is a consequence of their efforts to normalize pedophilia.

Homosexual activists have long justified pedophilia. Harry Hay is regarded as the founder of the gay rights movement. He not only endorsed sexual relations between adults and minors, but he also insisted the kids would love it. Larry Kramer, founder of ACT UP, a radical gay group with a penchant for violence, also maintained that "very often" children like having sex with adults.[134] Paul Shanley, the serial child rapist who was adored by Boston's liberal elites—he was their favorite priest, though he was eventually defrocked and sent to prison—liked to say that "the kid is the seducer."[135] Though there are heterosexuals who are child rapists as well, there is no prominent straight organization dedicated to justifying it. But homosexuals have NAMBLA.

[134] Bill Donohue, "Normalizing Pedophilia," Catholic League, January 12, 2022, https://www.catholicleague.org/normalizing/pedophilia/.
[135] Bill Donohue, *The Truth about Clergy Sexual Abuse* (San Francisco: Ignatius Press, 2021), 196.

It would be bad enough if men like these were confined to the fringes of society; but they are not. B4U-ACT is an organization of psychiatrists and other mental health professionals that seeks to normalize pedophilia. Founded in 2003, it is the originator of the term *minor-attracted persons* (known as MAPs), a sanitized term for pedophiles. Members of this organization are drawn from the most prestigious universities in the United States and Europe. Their goal is to convince the public that MAPs—they are almost all men—are seriously misunderstood and suffer primarily from being stigmatized by the rest of us.

B4U-ACT believes that pedophilia is not a sexual disorder: it is simply another sexual orientation. Its members take umbrage at the idea that MAPs are mentally disturbed; and some argue that it is nonsense to say that children are unable to consent to sex with adults. As one of their sages put it, "An adult's desire to have sex with children is 'normative.'"[136]

One of the founders of B4U-ACT was Michael Melsheimer, a former YMCA director who was sent to a federal prison for four years for sexually abusing kids. He committed suicide in 2010. When he died, B4U-ACT did not mention in his obituary that he was a child rapist.

It is astonishing how professional libertines always focus on children. If they are not physically molesting them, or encouraging others to do so, they are deliberately attempting to sexualize them with obscene and offensive ideas, often disguised as part of an educational experience.

[136] Donohue, "Normalizing Pedophilia."

One of the most popular, and indefensible, ways to sexualize children is to expose them to a Drag Queen Story Hour (DQSH). Amazingly, there are even some parents and grandparents who think this is a fun-loving way for kids to appreciate diversity. What could be wrong with men dressed as women reading to kids in the local library?

Upon closer inspection, it becomes quite clear that these events were founded to promote an agenda—namely, to normalize aberrant sexual behavior.

Tayler Hansen is an independent journalist who attended a drag queen Christmas show in Austin, Texas, in 2022. He was suspended by Twitter for sharing footage he took at the "all ages" event. At the "family-friendly" show, performers simulated sex, danced suggestively, and made sexual gestures to the audience, which included roughly twenty children.[137]

A particularly disturbing drag queen Christmas show took place in 2022 in Orlando, Florida, where children were in attendance. What was even more foul about it was the way the media sanitized the event. Three months after it occurred, the *Miami Herald* did a story on it that was almost surreal:

According to the *Herald*, the performance featured "shimmying, bare-chested men who wouldn't have been out of place at a Madonna concert."

Question: What kind of men shimmy half naked in front of children? Wouldn't pedophiles find this attractive?

---

[137] Ashley Carnahan, "Video of 'All Ages' Christmas Drag Show Sparks Outrage: 'These Children Are Being Groomed by Adults,'" Fox News, December 20, 2022, https://www.foxnews.com/media/video-all-ages-christmas-drag-show-sparks-outrage-children-being-groomed-adults/.

The performance featured men in "outfits [that were] provocative (bikinis and short shorts)."

Question: Why is it that these men like to parade around in public wearing the equivalent of a jock strap in front of kids? Is there something wrong with them? Pictures of them "performing" showed them almost entirely naked.

The performance did not show "exposure of genital organs."

Question: Why would this even have to be said if this were truly a typical children's event? Are we to celebrate their "modesty" for not exposing themselves? Normal men don't go to the grocery store dressed this way. Why is it okay at a children's event?

The performance showed a male actor, Jimbo the Clown, "giving birth to a log of bologna and throwing slices to the crowd." The scene was described by state agents, who videotaped what happened, as a "graphic depiction ... of childbirth and/or abortion." Also, there was "an image of a finger penetrating a wreath."

Question: Why are these freaks bent on putting sexual ideas, of a crude sort, into the minds of children? Do they have that little respect for childhood?

The performance included lyrics to their sick version of "Rudolph the Red-Nosed Reindeer" that were patently vulgar, even for adults, never mind kids: "You know Dasher and Dancer and Prancer and Vixen/Vomit and Stupid and Dildo and Dicks-in/But do you recall the most famous reindeer of all?/Screwdolph the Red-Nippled Reindeer had a very shiny bust."

Question: What would possess men to act this way? Are they mentally ill? Or just plain evil? Children as young as six were in attendance. And why did the Miami Herald *treat this insane event so casually?*[138]

DQSH was founded in San Francisco in 2015 by Michelle Tomasik, who goes by the name Michelle Tea.[139] Though she has no academic credentials—she never even went to college—her standing in the lesbian community earned her a post at Tulane University as a writer-in-residence. The goal of DQSH, she said, is to introduce kids to the "LGBTQ+ culture." She has been greatly assisted by the American Library Association (ALA) in achieving her goal. The ALA is run overwhelmingly by white women who are left-wing ideologues; a lesbian Marxist became president in July 2023.

The ALA is responsible for the spread of DQSH throughout the country; local libraries pay gays to run the events. A blog post on the ALA website once encouraged librarians to promote the LGBT agenda by "sneakily fit[ting] stuff in current programs."

One of the most popular books stocked by libraries is *The Gender Fairy*. It is meant for infants and toddlers. It tells

[138] Bill Donohue, "Drag Queen Vulgarity Is Child Abuse," Catholic League, March 22, 2023, https://www.catholicleague.org/drag-queen-vulgarity-is-child-abuse/.

[139] All of the following DQSH material is reported in Bill Donohue, "Drag Queen Story Hour Is Perverse," Catholic League, November 16, 2022, https://www.catholicleauge.org/drag-queen-story-hour-is-perverse/.

them that "only you know whether you are a boy or a girl. No one can tell you." That means parents, of course.

In 2018, videographer Sean Fitzgerald and the David Horowitz Freedom Center created a video showing teachers in grades K–12 bringing drag queens into schools to teach gender ideology. A teacher was caught telling her class, "It's okay to be different. There is no such thing as 'boy' or 'girl' things." The students were first graders.

What's going on? Why have these librarians and teachers become activists for the LGBT cause?

Lil Miss Hot Mess is one of the nation's leading drag queen authors and activists promoting DQSH. She says she loves it when kids realize "that things aren't necessarily the way they've always been told they have to be." Again, this is a clear shot at parents. Who are *they* to have told their children what's right and wrong?

Kevin Roberts is president of the Heritage Foundation. He is concerned about our culture creating a "new generation of drag kids." He's right. In the summer of 2022, a video emerged of a young girl gyrating to music at a drag show as adults tossed dollar bills at her. It got so bad at a Brooklyn gay bar a few years earlier that a reporter who covered a drag event said, "I left after seeing a child dance on stage for money at nighttime." And all of this is intentional.

In 2022, after a topless drag queen at a Miami bar sought to entertain a girl—she was "between three and five years old"—the performer boasted, "Children belong at drag shows!!!! Children deserve to see fun & expression &

freedom."[140] This is why another drag queen in Pennsylvania showed up shirtless to teach children how to spin on a stripper's pole at a Pride festival.

Tea may be the founder of DQSH, but its most famous intellectual advocate is Judith Butler. She is convinced that being male or female is merely a social construct and that sex is a fluid concept. The reason she likes drag queen events is that they deliberately confuse children. She coined a vulgar name ("genderf—k") to describe this phenomenon, proudly admitting that it is a "subversive" enterprise.[141] In other words, drag queen shows are intentionally done to confuse little children about the distinctions between males and females. If kids are persuaded that the traditional reality of a man and a woman is wrong, the next step to believing in gender fluidity is not very large.

The goal of confusing children about gender and sex was achieved by Blaine Banghart, an elementary school teacher in Shreveport, Louisiana. (He goes by MX instead of Mr. or Ms.) He bragged on Facebook about his success: "The kids are all confused and asking why I have a mustache if I'm a girl, if I'm Mr. Banghart now, why am I trying to look like a boy, etc." Responding to the way people reacted to him, he said, "I'm mostly just enjoying all the confusion

---

[140] Madeleine Kearns, "Children Belong at Drag Shows," *National Review*, July 5, 2022, www.nationalreview.com/corner/children-belong-at-drag-shows/.

[141] Helen Pluckrose and James Lindsay, *Cyclical Theories: How Atheist Scholarship Made Everything about Race, Gender, and Identity and Why This Harms Everybody* (Durham, NC: Pitchstone Publishing, 2020), 103.

about 'what' I am. Wondering what they're going to do when I have a mustache AND a skirt later this week lol."[142]

It is startling how many women are drawn to DQSH. Williams College professor Darel E. Paul explains that "drag's triumph over masculinity is a core element of its celebration of femininity, a celebration central to its appeal to straight women."[143] He relates how women brought their children to a "Drag Your Kids to Pride" event at a bar outside Dallas in 2022. Kids were told to "pass dollar bills to dancing drag queens under the glow of a four-foot-high neon sign blazoning the message, 'It's Not Gonna Lick Itself.'" He was awestruck by the mothers. "The willingness of mothers to endorse men's appropriating a female identity to engage in aggressive sexual vulgarity under the banner of tolerance is truly astonishing."[144]

Too bad these mothers don't heed the warnings of drag queen Kitty Demure. What he had to say to parents is worth repeating: "I have no idea why you want drag queens to read books to your children.... What in the hell has a drag queen ever done to make you have so much respect for them and admire them so much? Other than put on makeup and jump on the floor and writhe around and do sexual things on stage? I have absolutely no idea why you would want that to

---

[142] Charlotte Bond, "Teacher Says It's Enjoyable Confusing Kids about Gender," *Daily Wire*, December 6, 2022, https://www.dailywire.com/news/teacher-says-its-enjoyable-confusing-kids-about-gender/.

[143] Darel E. Paul, "Drag Queens," *First Things*, February 2023, 38.

[144] Ibid., 40.

influence your child. Would you want a stripper or a porn star to influence your child?"

Demure wasn't finished with his reality check. "A drag queen performs in a nightclub for adults. There is a lot of filth that goes on, a lot of sexual stuff that goes on. And backstage there's a lot of nudity, sex, and drugs.... So I don't think this is an avenue you would want your child to explore.... But to actually get [your children] involved in drag is extremely, extremely irresponsible on your part."[145]

If more parents heard what this drag queen had to say, they might think twice about exposing their children to such fare. It is not a sign of tolerance to take kids to DQSH. It's a sign of moral bankruptcy.

---

[145] Donohue, "Drag Queen Story Hour Is Perverse."

CHAPTER 4

TRANSGENDERISM

THE SECULAR-RELIGIOUS DEBATE
OVER TRANSGENDERISM

In 2017, one of the most famous soccer players who ever played the game, Vasilis Tsiartas, posted a social media message about transgenderism. The retired eighteen-year soccer star said, "God created Adam and Eve. The rest [of gender identities] were manufactured for consumption." At the end of 2022, the Greek legend was jailed for ten months and fined 5,000 euros by a court in Athens for his "offense."[146]

Courts can punish Christians, but they cannot change the Bible. "God created mankind in his image; in the image of God he created them; male and female he created them." This Genesis account (1:27) is augmented by the book of Wisdom, which notes that God made man in "the

---

[146] Ben Johnson, "Sports Star to Be Jailed 10 Months for 'Transphobic' Message That 'God Created Adam and Eve,'" Daily Signal, November 10, 2022, https://www.dailysignal.com/.

image of his own nature" (2:23). These quotes from Scripture are not simply observations; their significance extends to the social order.

The influential Jewish scholar Harry Jaffa maintained that the root of all morality was nature. "The distinction between a man and a woman is a distinction as fundamental as any in nature, because it is the very distinction by which nature itself is constituted."[147]

Jaffa wrote this to show how homosexuality strikes at the authority and dignity of the family. But transgenderism threatens the family in a similar fashion. Transgenderism is not just an idea. It is an ideology. To be exact, it is a set of ideas that provide a comprehensive account of man and society. By rejecting the reality of male and female, these ideologues would create a world that has no meaning—but that, ironically, they want us to believe in.

The tenets of Christianity and transgenderism are polar opposites that cannot be reconciled. Pope Francis understands this as well as anyone. He calls gender ideology "one of the most dangerous ideological colonizations" of our time. "Why is it dangerous? Because it blurs the differences and the value of men and women."[148] So upset

[147] Harry V. Jaffa, *Homosexuality and the Natural Law*, (n.p.: Claremont Institute, 1990), 33.

[148] "Pope Francis: Gender Ideology Is 'One of the Most Dangerous Ideological Colonizations' Today," *National Catholic Register*, March 11, 2023, https://ncregister.com/cna/pope-francis-ideological-colonization-today/.

was Pope Francis with transgenderism that he once called it "demonic."[149]

Male and Female He Created Them is the Vatican's most authoritative statement on transgenderism. By denying human nature and "the reciprocity of a man and a woman," transgenderism seeks to eliminate "the anthropological basis of the family."[150] Furthermore, "the concept of gender is seen as dependent upon the subjective mindset of each person, who can choose a gender not corresponding to his or her biological sex, and therefore with the way others see that person (*transgenderism*)."[151] The Church recognizes how absurd such a contention is, if for no other reason than it denies the obvious. "The physiological *complementarity* of male-female sexual difference assures the necessary conditions for procreation."[152]

The absurdity of transgenderism has not been lost on Dennis Prager either. He takes his Judaism seriously, and that allows him to explain the ideology of transgenderism as an expression of secular thought. "It is a secular axiom that secularism and secular people are rooted in reason, whereas religion and the religious are rooted in irrationality." But he

[149] Pope Francis made this comment to Austrian bishop Andreas Laun. It was reported by John-Henry Westen, "Austrian Bishop: Pope Francis Told Me 'Gender Ideology is Demonic,'" Life Site News, January 30, 2014, https://www.lifesitenews.com/news/austrian-bishop-pope-francis-told-me-gender-ideology-is-demonic/.

[150] Congregation for Catholic Education, *"Male and Female He Created Them": Towards a Path of Dialogue on the Question of Gender Theory in Education* (Vatican City, 2019), 3.

[151] Ibid., 8.

[152] Ibid., 14.

makes mincemeat of this popular supposition by providing a few examples.[153]

✠ "Only secular people believe 'men give birth.'"

✠ "Only secular people believe that males — providing, of course, that they say they are females — should be allowed to compete in women's sports."

✠ "Only secular people believe that a young girl who says she is a boy or a young boy who says he is a girl should be given puberty-blocking hormones."

✠ "Only secular people believe that girls who say they are boys should have their healthy breasts surgically cut off."

✠ "Only secular people believe it is good to have men in drag dance (often provocatively) in front of 5-year-olds."

There are many other such examples. Some of those who work at Harvard Medical School now refer to mothers and women as "birthing persons."[154] Similarly, the sages at the

[153] Dennis Prager, "Who's More Irrational — the Religious or the Irreligious?," Heartland Daily News, January 24, 2023, https://heartlanddailynews.com/2023/01/dennis-prager-whos-more-irrational-the-religious-or-the-irreligoius/.

[154] John Kass, "Why Are We Calling Mothers 'Birthing Persons'?," Baltimore Sun, June 21, 2021, https://www.baltimoresun.com/opinion/op-ed/bs-ed-0621-katz-birthing-mothers-20210621-4lvc7jtpnrd37ci24oikwattc4-a-story-html/.

ACLU are convinced that "men who get pregnant and give birth are men."[155] They did not say if they can miscarry.

In 2023, Johns Hopkins University redefined what a lesbian is, calling her "a non-man attracted to non-men," thereby effectively erasing women.[156] Matt Walsh, who has had lots of fun making fools of these true believers, recalls that in his research on this subject he interviewed an administrator at a school where "students identified as cats, and teachers affirmed them as cats."[157]

Sometimes sarcasm is the only thing that seems to jolt these ideologues out of their twilight zone. If the subject of transgenderism comes up when I am doing radio or TV, I often say, "Most people think I'm a big Irishman. Wrong. I'm a Chinese dwarf. I'm self-identifying." That ends the discussion.

Denying reality is so common among professors that they are losing the respect of their students. When a professor of anthropology at the University of Pittsburgh was asked, "If you were to dig up a human—two humans—a hundred years from now, both a man and a woman, could you tell the difference strictly off of bones?" Incredibly, he answered,

---

[155] "ACLU Claims 'Men Who Get Pregnant and Give Birth Are Men,'" Fox News, November 20, 2019, https://www.foxnews.com/media/aclu-men-pregnant-periods/.

[156] Simon Kent, "J. K. Rowling Rips Johns Hopkins University for Labeling Lesbians as 'A Non-man Attracted to Non-men,'" Breitbart, June 14, 2023, https://www.brietbart.com/entertainment/2023/06/14/j.k-rowling-rips-johns-hopkins-university-for-labeling-lesbians-as-a-non-man-attracted-to-non-men/.

[157] Gillian Richards, "Gender Ideology Is 'Half-Baked, Incoherent,' Filmmaker Matt Walsh Tells Full House at Catholic University," Daily Signal, October 6, 2022, https://www.dailysignal.com/.

"No," despite the fact that differences in the pelvis are clearly determined by sex. The students erupted in laughter.[158]

Sometimes those who play this politically correct game don't believe the nonsense they are promoting themselves. At the U.S. Air Force Academy, students learn about "agender," "bigender," "two-spirit," and "demigender" people. When the head of the academy, Lt. Gen. Richard M. Clark, was asked at a congressional hearing what *agender* and *demigender* mean, he answered, "I'm not really sure."[159] But that did not stop him from defending this insanity.

At another congressional hearing, the president of the Human Rights Campaign, Kelley Robinson, was asked, "Is there a difference between women and men?" The head of the supreme LGBT organization in the nation dodged the question over and over, refusing to offer a clear-cut answer. She was then asked, "Why do women's sports exist?" Again, she could not provide a coherent answer.[160] Had she given an honest answer, she knew it would have demonstrated that there is (obviously) a difference between a man and a woman—and she couldn't do that.

[158] Natalie O'Neill, "'Woke' University of Pittsburgh Professor Denies Difference in Male, Female Skeleton," *New York Post*, March 31, 2023, https://nypost.com/2023/03/31/woke-professor-denies-male-female-skeleton-differences/.

[159] Elizabeth Elkind, "Gaetz Stumps Air Force General on Gender Identity Labels: 'I'm Not Really Sure,'" Fox News, July 19, 2023, https://www.foxnews.com/politics/gaetz-air-force-general-identity-labels/.

[160] Senator Ted Cruz questioned her on June 21, 2023, at a Senate Judiciary Committee hearing on transgender rights. See https://twitter.com/therecountstatus/1671563147902332928.

The madness of our age was spotlighted by two professors, Peter Boghossian, a philosophy professor at Portland State University in Oregon, and author James Lindsay, who has a Ph.D. in mathematics. Using fake names and a fictitious research institute, they submitted a paper to a peer-reviewed journal, *Cogent Social Sciences,* that was a hoax. It was published. The title of their piece was "The Conceptual Penis as a Social Construct." That's right, the distinguished editors of this scholarly journal were persuaded that "the conceptual penis is better understood not as an anatomical organ but as a social construct isomorphic to performative toxic masculinity."[161] The authors made up the fanciful jargon to make it sound credible to these savants.

While this level of absurdity is easily mocked, it is not funny to read about the draconian measures taken against those who don't cooperate in this madness.

Korean-style spas for women require nudity. When a man, who identified as a woman, was turned away from entering a Korean spa in Seattle, he filed a complaint with the Washington State Human Rights Commission. The spa owners told the state agency that because of their Christian beliefs, they don't believe men and women should see each other naked outside of marriage. The commission was not swayed and ordered the spa to allow the man to enter.[162]

---

[161] "Hoax Article Claiming the Penis Is a Social Construct Gets Published in Scholarly Journal," Impact News Service, May 22, 2017.

[162] Katrina Trinko, "In 2023, Forcing Women to See Penises Isn't Sexual Harassment—It's the Law," Daily Signal, June 9, 2023, https://www.dailysignal.com.

A similar incident occurred in Los Angeles at another Korean spa. After a man disrobed in the women's area — thereby displaying his genitals to young girls, teens, and adult women — he was ordered to leave. He filed a complaint, and protesters even showed up at the spa to defend him. (The police arrested several dozen of them, taking away a stun gun, knives, and pepper spray.[163])

When two students in a California school "misgendered" their teacher — referring to the female teacher who identified as a man as a female — they were suspended for five days and forced to attend a "restorative justice" training program as punishment.[164]

When a Vermont high school teacher told his snowboarding team that biological males have a physical advantage over female-born athletes, he was fired for sharing his views (which were accurate) on transgender athletes.[165]

But get this: in a 2023 survey, 44 percent of those between the ages of twenty-five and thirty-four believe that

---

[163] Paul Best, "Antifa Violently Clashes with Police outside Los Angeles Spa following Alleged Transgender Disrobing Incident," Fox News, July 17, 2021, https//www.foxnews.com/us/los-angeles-spa-becomes-scene-of-protests-following-alleged-transgender-disrobing-incident/.

[164] Reagan Reese, "School Suspended Kids for 'Misgendering' Teacher, Sent Them to 'Restorative Justice' Training," Daily Caller, July 7, 2023, https://www.dailycaller.com/2023/07/07/school-suspended-kids-misgendering-justice-training/.

[165] Snejana Farberov, "Coach Sues School after Being Fired over His Views on Trans Athletes," New York Post, July 20, 2023, https://nypost.com/2023/07/20/vermont-coach-sues-school-after-being-fired-over-trans-views/.

"referring to someone by the wrong gender pronoun should be a criminal offense." Criminalizing such speech is also approved by 38 percent of those between the ages of thirty-five and forty-four.[166] What madness.

ORIGINS OF TRANSGENDERISM

The notion that we can switch our sex is a classic example of postmodernism. After all, if truth is a fiction, then why shouldn't any idea, no matter how fallacious, be entertained as real? Except, when NBC News did a story on people who claim to be able to change their race, it created a firestorm. But why? It shouldn't have, certainly not among those who claim we can change our sex.

If self-identity is dispositive for sex—which is precisely what gender ideology maintains—why isn't that true for race? In other words, if a male claims to be female, why can't someone of one race claim to be that of another, if all that matters is self-identification?

NBC's experts claimed there is a dramatic difference. Race, they said, is purely a social construct with no basis in biology. But that is what gender ideology holds as well. So if both race and sex are social constructs, why can we change our sex but not our race? The logic implodes.

The fact is, there are biological and social aspects to both race and sex, meaning that nature determines our race and sex, and social norms determine how we respond to them. Those who maintain that we can change our sex but not our race do so because it sustains their belief that our sexual identity is a fluid concept. But if white people can claim to be black, this would create havoc for the victimology industry, and that is not a prospect the Left can endure.[167]

If philosophers created postmodern thought, it was the sexologists who applied such thought and really put it on the map.

The term *gender* is actually a sociological term that describes the social roles appropriate for males and females; the term *sex* is a biological term that describes the nature-based differences between a man and a woman. Typically, gender roles take their cues from nature. But this is something that secularists try to deny. More important, they reject the very existence of nature, and hold that every biological difference between men and women is merely a made-up social construct. They are wrong, of course. But this is what happens when the existence of God and nature are denied.

The pervert-scientist Alfred Kinsey was among the first to deconstruct the anthropological basis of human sexuality. But it was left to Dr. John Money, a psychology professor at Johns Hopkins University, to redefine gender and claim that it was nothing more than a social construct that facilitated our sexual identity.

---

[167] Bill Donohue, "If We Can Change Our Sex, Why Not Our Race?," September 26, 2023, Catholic League, https://www. catholicleague.org/if-we-can-change-our-sex-why-not-our-race/.

In the 1950s, Money argued that if a child is uncomfortable with his sex, his parents should treat him as if he were the opposite sex. He meant what he said, even to the point of telling the parents of a boy who had had his penis disfigured in a botched circumcision to raise him as a girl, under his supervision. The boy, David Reimer, had an identical twin, which was seen by Money as a godsend: he could test his wacky theories, using David as a guinea pig. David's parents unfortunately agreed, and sex reassignment surgery was performed. David became known as Brenda. Following the advice of Money, his parents never told their "daughter" that he was born a boy.

Money's abusive experiment was a flop. David was never happy "being" a girl, and eventually his parents told him the truth. He underwent additional surgery, this time in an effort to restore his nature-given sex. He was renamed David, but even after all the hormone treatments, he was never able to function as a male. He subsequently committed suicide.[168] His tragic case shows how stubborn human nature is, and how wrong transgenderists are.

Money, like Kinsey, was a pedophile. He was a consultant to the *Journal of Paedophilia*, a publication that sought to introduce children to pornography and to normalize man-boy sex. Money also argued in favor of eliminating the age of consent, and even went so far as to say there should be no penalty for death arising from consensual

---

[168] Abigail Shrier, *Irreversible Damage: The Transgender Craze Seducing Our Daughters* (Washington, D.C.: Regnery Publishing, 2020), 119–120.

rough sex. Not surprisingly, he wanted to legalize incest and sex with children.

In other words, the origins of transgenderism are traceable to sexperts who promoted child abuse.

But transgenderism could never have succeeded without the backing of contemporary feminists. The original feminists, such as Elizabeth Cady Stanton and Susan B. Anthony, fought for the equal treatment of women in society and an end to discrimination in the workplace. These nineteenth-century advocates for equality had little in common with the feminists of the 1960s. The feminists of the '60s were more consumed with sex than anything else. They embraced abortion and lesbianism as their cherished goals. Modern feminists are even worse: today, "feminists" work *against* women's rights, and they insist that men who identify as women should be permitted to compete in women's sports.

The National Organization for Women was founded in 1966 as the premier women's rights organization. Today it is working overtime to support men who claim to be women to compete in women's sports. As a result, men like Will Thomas, who calls himself Lia, are allowed to compete against women. In 2022, he won the NCAA championship in women's swimming.

Christina Hoff Sommers is one of the few women scholars who have taken aim at contemporary feminists. She notes that today's feminists draw on angry and resentful young women for support, convincing them of their "oppressed" condition. They are anti-male, and like the postmodernists, they recoil at the idea that truth and facts exist. Thus, they are easily seduced by the fiction of transgenderism.

Kara Dansky is directly involved in debunking the myths of transgenderism. She is a "leftist and a Democrat" whose feminist credentials are impeccable. But she is also someone who is appalled at the transgender movement, which, she says, is undercutting the advancements that women have achieved.

When men are allowed to parade around naked in a women's spa, she notes, and are in fact defended by women's advocates, the rights of women are being eviscerated in a really sick way. "This assault on women's sex-based rights is not occurring in a vacuum or by accident," she writes. "It is being perpetrated by a vicious and brutal industry that operates openly and yet manages to sneak under the public radar. Its aim is to abolish sex in the law and throughout society. We are all victims of this assault, but those most harmed are women and girls, i.e., female human beings."[169]

Dansky has little in common with Simone de Beauvoir, the twentieth-century French intellectual who endorsed the ideological grounds of transgenderism before almost anyone had heard of it. De Beauvoir believed that human nature was a fiction and that our lives were without meaning. What exists is not what nature has ordained; it is what we have created. Reality is an ongoing enterprise, she said, and it is entirely constructed by what we do. To the extent that men and women exist at all, their makeup is socially devised.

---

[169] Kara Dansky, *The Abolition of Sex: How the "Transgender" Agenda Harms Women and Girls* (New York: Bombardier, 2021), 5.

De Beauvoir set the intellectual table for transgender scholars such as Judith Butler.

Butler breathed new life into de Beauvoir's bizarre notion that "one is not born, but rather becomes, a woman." For Butler, it is the perception that someone is a male or female that counts; there is no such thing as a "real" sex. Moreover, gender is only a performance, and it is nonsense to say women exist. It's all in your head.

Abigail Favale is correct to note that Butler's "primary goal as a theorist is to dismantle the normalization of heterosexual relationships—the tendency to see the male and female sexual relationship as normal and natural, which in theory-speak is called *heteronormativity.*"[170]

It is hardly surprising to learn that Butler is a lesbian who prefers to be called "they." Her writing is so vague and incoherent that it is hard to understand what in the world she is talking about. Perhaps she likes it that way. One of her more storied articles was titled "The Lesbian Phallus." She spent her younger years "as a bar dyke" who read Hegel during the day while spending her evenings "at the gay bar."[171] She has long been active in gay and lesbian circles, as well as in a host of radical left-wing causes. Oppression is ubiquitous, she contends, casting "racism, misogyny, homophobia, transphobia [and] capitalism" as its primary generators.[172]

[170] Abigail Favale, *The Genesis of Gender: A Christian Theory* (San Francisco: Ignatius Press, 2022), 12, 72–73.

[171] Angela Franks, "Judith Butler's Trouble," *First Things*, May 2023, 43.

[172] "Judith Butler: 'We Need to Rethink the Category of Woman,'" *Guardian*, September 7, 2021, https://www.theguardian.com/

We have come a long way from the days when Margaret Mead, the famous anthropologist, stunned her followers by declaring that patriarchy was real and universal. To this day, radical feminists lie about her work, and assert that she concluded that there were no inherent differences between men and women and that it was culture, not nature, that accounted for male supremacy.

While it is true that in her early writings Mead gave credence to that position, she later revised her thinking: "Nowhere do I suggest that I have found any material which disproves the existence of sex differences." In fact, she insisted that there had never been a single society where women ruled. "Men have always been the leaders in public affairs and the final authorities at home."[173]

Mead carries weight precisely because she was no conservative. She was married three times to men, but spent more time in her relationship with a woman lover.

PROFILE OF TRANS PERSONS

According to a 2022 Pew survey, 1.6 percent of U.S. adults claim to be transgender. Three percent of adults between the ages of eighteen and twenty-nine say they are non-binary and 2 percent said they are transgender, but only .3 percent of those fifty years old or older make such a claim. Furthermore, in 2023, a Gallup poll found that within Generation Z, the LGBT population doubled in just four years, from 10.5 percent in

---

lifeandstyle/2021/sep/07/judith-butler-interview-gender/.

[173] Bill Donohue, *Common Sense Catholicism: How to Resolve Our Cultural Crisis* (San Francisco: Ignatius Press, 2019), 129.

2017 to 20.8 percent in 2021; for the nation as a whole, 7.2 percent of adults said they are LGBT. In other words, the dramatic increase in claims of sexual abnormality demonstrates that we are witnessing a culturally induced disorder.

One Ivy League institution, Brown University, is so engulfed in transgenderism that between 2010 and 2023, the gay and lesbian population increased by 26 percent, and the percentage identifying as bisexual increased by 232 percent. Those identifying as "other sexual orientations" within the LGBT population increased by almost 800 percent. In 2023, almost four in ten students (38 percent) identified as LGBTQI+.

If anyone doubts that this is a culturally induced condition, consider that young people in California, one of the most liberal states in the country, are 40 percent more likely to identify as transgender than the national average.

Transgenderism is flowering in colleges because the professors are almost all in the secular camp. There is nothing new about that. But what is new is the attack on science coming from this august quarter.

One of the more popular gender myths is the assertion that gender is "assigned." Besides being a misuse of the term — *sex* is the proper word — it is manifestly untrue that our sex is "assigned." Our sex is determined by our father, and our father alone. Society has nothing to do with it. Our sex may be recorded by a hospital staffer. But it is never "assigned" by anyone.

Our imaginations are fertile. We can certainly imagine being the opposite sex — or a different species, for that matter. But subjective descriptions of our identity are not dispositive. What matters is reality. And the reality is that we cannot change our chromosomal makeup. Men are XY and women are XX.

Proponents of transgenderism like to say that there are "intersex" persons, meaning there are people born with both male and female genitalia. This is true. There is also a biological disorder that affects boys called Klinefelter syndrome (XXY). But so what? Even in those rare chromosomal configurations, all of those people are either male or female.

Fr. Tad Pacholczyk has a doctorate in neuroscience from Yale and did postdoctoral work at Harvard. "For the most part," he says, "our genetic makeup (XX female or XY male) serves as the best guide to the true sex of an individual, though in rare situations, even the sex chromosomes themselves can have anomalies." He mentions Klinefelter syndrome as an example. However, even those born with "confounding physiological factors," he says, are either intrinsically male or female. In other words, humans are "marked by sexual 'dimorphism,' or 'two-forms,' namely, male or female. When problems arise in the development of one of those forms, this does not make for a new 'third form,' or worse, for an infinite spectrum of different sexual forms."[174]

Anti-science transgender activists are among the most intolerant people in our society. They believe that there are

[174] Fr. Tad Pacholczyk, "Making Sense of Bioethics: Column 132: Seeing through the Intersex Confusion," National Catholic Bioethics Center, June 2016, www.ncbcenter.org.

more than two sexes, and anyone who disagrees—which is to say, most normal people—is dismissed as "transphobic." For example, when the famous atheist Richard Dawkins said the obvious, "sex really is binary," he was slammed by his fellow atheists. But Dawkins is a biologist, not a pundit. His critics nearly fell off the cliff when he offered this pedestrian definition of a woman: "A woman is an adult human female, free of Y chromosomes." They accused him of "transphobia."[175]

WHAT "TRANSITIONING" ENTAILS

Once a young person "transitions," he or she often becomes an instant celebrity. "Being trans is a gold star in the eyes of other teens" is how one respondent put it in a scientific study.[176] But for how long? The evidence shows that the initial rush that is experienced is typically followed by a long series of problems, some of which can be deadly.

In 2022, California became a "sanctuary state" for trans youth. Boys and girls who are sexually confused, and live in states where puberty blockers and chemical castration are considered child abuse, can go to California where they are "treated." The governor, Gavin Newsom—who helped kill

[175] Hemant Mehta, "Richard Dawkins Has Abandoned Science to Justify His Transphobia," Religion News Service, August 1, 2023, https://religionnews.com/2023/08/01/richard-dawkins-has-abandoned-science-to-justify-his-transphobia/.

[176] Lisa Littman, "Parent Reports of Adolescents and Young Adults Perceived to Show Signs of a Rapid Onset of Gender Dysphoria," *PLOS ONE* 13, no. 8 (August 16, 2018): e0202330, https://doi.org/10.1371/journal.pone.0202330.

his own mother in 2002, when assisted suicide was a felony—signed the legislation.[177] A month before he signed it, lawmakers heard testimony against it. But it made no difference. One of those who testified was Chloe Cole, an eighteen-year-old girl who described what happened to her when she was fifteen.

She told the legislators that she was placed on puberty blockers and testosterone after expressing gender dysphoria to her therapist. Her parents went along with this because they were told there were only two choices: either she transitions or she will kill herself. Chloe asked the legislators, "Who here really believes that as a fifteen-year-old, I should have had my healthy breasts removed or that should have been an option?" She predicted that the bill would "open the floodgate for confused children like me to get the gender interventions that so many regret. I am the canary in the coal mine."[178]

In 2023, Chloe testified before Congress. "I used to believe that I was born in the wrong body and the adults in my life, whom I trusted, affirmed my belief, and this caused me lifelong, irreversible harm. I speak to you today as a victim of one of the biggest medical scandals in the history of the United States." After recounting her incredible experiences, she pleaded with the lawmakers to change course. "We need to stop telling children that puberty is an option, that they can choose what kind of puberty they will go

[177] Bill Donohue, "Newsom's Latest Sanctuary State Scam," Catholic League, September 30, 2022, https//www.catholicleague.org/newsoms-latest-sanctuary-state-scam/.
[178] Ibid.

through, just like they can choose what clothes to wear or what music to listen to."[179]

President Biden is working to undermine Chloe. He is strongly opposed to state laws that ban minors from undergoing sex-reassignment surgery, saying they should not have the right to do so. But the public is on Chloe's side. In fact, 62 percent strongly support legislation making it illegal to perform sex-change surgery on minors.[180] A majority, 55 percent, say it is "morally wrong" to transition to the opposite sex.[181] And a growing number of Americans, seven in ten, say that biological men should not be allowed to compete in women's sports.[182]

It looks like the public is far ahead of the Biden administration. The evidence is mounting that the public is right.

At the end of 2022, a study was released in the United Kingdom on this subject: "The 'gender-affirming' model of

[179] Chloe Cole, "Detransitioner Chloe Cole's Full Testimony to Congress Is a 'Final Warning' to Stop Gender Surgery," *New York Post*, July 29, 2023, https://nypost.com/2023/07/28/detransitioner-chloe-coles-full-testimony-to-congress-is-a-final-warning-to-stop-gender-sugery/.

[180] Craig Bannister, "Across the Board, Americans Reject Transgender Ideology, Especially When It Threatens Minors," *MRCTV*, June 2, 2023, https:mrctv.org/blog/across-board-americans-reject-transgender-ideology-especially-when-it-threatens-minors/.

[181] Sarah Prentice, "Trends Show Americans Transitioning Away from Transgender Ideology," *MRCTV*, June 23, 2023, https://mrctv.org/blog/trends-show-americans-transitioning-away-transgender-ideology#/.

[182] Jeffrey Jones, "More Say Gender Should Dictate Sports Participation," Gallup, June 12, 2023, https://news.gallup.com/poll/507023/say-birth-gender-dictate-sports-participation.aspx/.

care for teenagers is based on evidence that falls apart under examination. There is strong evidence that this medical pathway causes physical harm. It can lead to infertility and loss of future sexual function; among multiple side effects, bone health suffers."[183]

The Mayo Clinic has published a long list of physical problems that follow transitioning. The list should be given, by law, to every person, minor or adult, who is considering such a change. For men who take female hormones, they may expect blood clots, high triglycerides, weight gain, infertility, high potassium, high blood pressure, type 2 diabetes, cardiovascular disease, stroke, and increased breast cancer. For women who transition, many of the same conditions can be expected, along with a drier and thinner vagina, pelvic pain, clitoral discomfort, and vaginal atrophy.[184]

There is a reason why the Food and Drug Administration has approved medications to treat prostate cancer, endometriosis, and other diseases, but has never approved them for gender dysphoria, the clinical term used to describe the belief that one's body is the wrong sex. There is a mountain of evidence that puberty blockers do great harm,

[183] Breccan F. Thies, "Study: 'Gender-Affirming Care' for Children Has No Basis in Medicine," Breitbart, December 27, 2022, https://breitbart.com/politics/2022/12/27/study-gender-affirming-care-for-children-has-no-basis-in-medicine/.

[184] Bill Donohue, "Transgender Report Part II: Physical Damage," Catholic League, August 24, 2021, https://www.catholicleague.org/transgender-report-part-ii-physical-damage/.

effectively locking children and young people in for a lifetime of further treatments.

Some of the techniques implemented to assist in transitioning are downright diabolical. A Canadian man who sought to transition to a female had doctors create an imitation vagina out of his inverted penis. The result was that his "neo-vagina" turned out to be an open wound that needed to be dilated daily to prevent it from closing. The pain was so excruciating that he requested the doctors to inject him with a lethal substance, putting him out of his physiological and psychological misery.

Most Americans would be startled to learn how easy it is to get approval to transition from one sex to the other. In an undercover investigation, Matt Walsh revealed that he and his team learned of a case where a man asked for an orchiectomy, a procedure to remove his testicles. It took just a twenty-two-minute virtual appointment to get the okay.[185]

Dr. Meredithe McNamara is a professor of pediatrics at Yale School of Medicine. She is a big supporter of transitioning. In 2023, she testified before Congress about a bill that eliminates federal funding for hospitals that provided sex-change procedures for minors. She was asked to cite

---

[185] Zach Jewell, "Matt Walsh Undercover Investigation Catches Trans Health Care Providers 'Rubber-Stamping' Sex-Change Surgeries," *Daily Wire*, June 7, 2023, https://www.dailywire.com/news/matt-walsh-undercover-investigation-catches-trans-health-care-providers-falsifying-patient-info-to-fast-track-sex-change-surgeries/.

scientific journal articles that showed that sex-reassignment surgery is beneficial. She could not name one.[186]

Despite the mounting evidence that transitioning is fraught with danger, some doctors continue to "treat" children as young as two and three years of age. Boston Hospital brags, "We see a variety of young children all the way down to ages 2 and 3."[187] The Gender and Sexuality Development Program at the Children's Hospital of Philadelphia has offered puberty blockers to children as young as eight.[188] The World Professional Association for Transgender Health announced new guidelines in 2022 calling for the removal of age minimums for children ready to embark on genital mutilation procedures.[189] In a sane world, these medical professionals would be jailed.

[186] Corey Walker, "'Name One': Dem Witness Deflects Question on Providing Studies Showing Benefits of Trans Procedures for Children," *Daily Caller*, June 14, 2023, https://dailycaller.com/2023/06/14/dem-witness-question-benefits-trans-procedures-children-dan-crenshaw/.

[187] Zachary Faria, "At Boston Children's Hospital, Illogical and Destructive Gender Ideology Reigns," *Washington Examiner*, August 15, 2022, www.washingtonexaminer.com/opinion/at-boston-childrens-hospital-illogical-and-destructive-gender-ideology/.

[188] Megan Brock and Laurel Duggan, "'Age Is a Number': Gender Clinic Offered Puberty Blockers to Kids as Young as 8, Surgery Referrals at 14, Records Show," *Daily Caller*, April 2, 2023, https://dailycaller.com/2023/04/02/gender-clinic-puberty-blockers-chop-pennsylvania/.

[189] Breccan F. Thies, "Avoiding Malpractice Lawsuits: Transgender Health Group Admits Reason for Removing Age Minimums for Genital Mutilation, Chemical Castration," Breitbart, September 20, 2022, https://breitbart.com/politics/2022/09/20/avoiding-malpractice-lawsuits-transgender-health-group-admits-reason-removing-age-minimums-genital-mutilation-chemical-castration/.

Erica Anderson is a transgender psychologist who has helped hundreds of teenagers to transition. A transgender person himself, he now thinks that "this has gone too far. It's going to get worse. I don't want any part of it."[190]

While much of the discussion centers on those who have transitioned, the plight of those who seek to detransition deserves our attention.

Chris Beck was a Navy SEAL who transitioned to "become" Kristin Beck; he later transitioned back. He went public with his story. His interviewer summarized their discussion, explaining "how the VA provided doctor convinced him he was trans in a 1 hr session, how the VA doctor hatched a deal to release a book together, how CNN used him and most importantly, to warn the children who could be harmed next." Admitting he was naïve, he said he was "propagandized" and "used badly by a lot of people."[191]

The rush to transition is not at all uncommon; and it is also one of the most irresponsible aspects of this entire enterprise. If someone told a doctor he wanted his healthy left leg removed, no physician would agree to do so. Yet if a man asks to have his genitals removed, more than a few doctors would jump at the opportunity.

[190] Lee Brown, "Trans Doctor Who Helps Teens Transition Says It's Now 'Gone Too Far,'" *New York Post*, April 15, 2022, http://nypost.com/2022/04/15/transitions-have-gone-too-far-trans-psychologist/.

[191] "Famous Transgender Navy SEAL Chris Beck Announces Detransition, Calls for Treatments on Kids to Stop," *Daily Caller*, December 1, 2022, https://dailycaller.com/2022/12/01/famous-transgender-navy-seal-chris-beck-announces-detransition-calls-treatments-kids-stop/.

In 2023, Michelle Zacchigna became the first detransitioner to file a lawsuit in Canada against medical providers. She claims they failed to address her mental health problems, allowed her to self-diagnose her condition, and permitted her to undergo irreversible procedures that she later regretted. The doctor she met referred her for male hormone therapy after a single hour-long appointment. The therapist she was seeing also recommended hormone therapy, despite knowing she had a long history of mental illness.[192] In other words, the people who were charged with her care failed to exercise responsible judgment.

Camille Kiefel never thought she might not actually be a woman until she enrolled at Portland State University and took a series of gender studies courses. In 2020, she had her breasts removed after just two hour-long Zoom meetings. Less than three years later, she sued her social worker, her therapist, and the gender clinics they worked for in Oregon. Fortunately, she was later able to see things clearly and started the process of detransitioning. "There's no third sex out there. It's just based on a feeling that this would be a good fit for you. It's a designer surgery but I didn't think of it at the time." She concluded, "It's weird Frankenstein surgery that they're doing."[193]

[192] "Detransitioner Files First Lawsuit in Canada against Medical Providers," *Daily Wire*, February 21, 2023, https://www.dailywire.com/news/detransitioner-files-first-lawsuit-in-canada-against-medical-providers/.

[193] Rikki Schlott, "Detransitioner: 'I'm Suing the Doctors Who Removed My Healthy Breasts,'" *New York Post*, December 3, 2022, https//nypost.com/2022/12/03/detransitioiner-im-suing-the-doctors-who-removed-my-healthy-breasts/.

MENTAL HEALTH ISSUES

If there is one person who has spent his life studying trans persons, it is Dr. Paul McHugh. He is the former psychiatrist-in-chief at Johns Hopkins Hospital and its current Distinguished Service Professor of Psychiatry. He was one of the pioneers in researching sex-reassignment surgery, and his several decades of work have documented the serious mental disorders from which people who underwent this surgery suffer. The suicide rate alone, he says, is twenty times that of comparable peers. His work with one of his colleagues, Dr. Lawrence S. Mayer, a psychiatrist at Johns Hopkins School of Medicine, led to a profound and definitive conclusion: "The hypothesis that gender identity is an innate, fixed property of human beings that is independent of biological sex — that a person might be 'a man trapped in a woman's body' or 'a woman trapped in a man's body' — is not supported by scientific evidence."[194]

McHugh maintains that transgender persons suffer from mental disorders in two ways. "The first is that the idea of sex misalignment is simply mistaken — it does not correspond with physical reality. The second is that it can lead to grim psychological outcomes." He compares their assumption that they are different from the physical reality of their body to a "dangerously thin" woman suffering

[194] Lawrence S. Mayer and Paul R. McHugh, "Sexuality and Gender: Findings from the Biological, Psychological, and Social Sciences," *New Atlantis*, no. 50 (Fall 2016): 8.

from anorexia who looks in the mirror and thinks she is "overweight."[195]

There is nothing natural about being a trans person — in fact, trans persons are rebelling against their nature — so it is hardly surprising to learn that they are almost always very unhappy people. In a 2023 large-scale KFF/*Washington Post* survey of transgender persons, researchers asked questions about their mental health that were then compared to the general population. The results were enlightening.[196]

✛ When asked about their childhood, 81 percent of all adults surveyed said it was either a very happy or a somewhat happy time; only 53 percent of trans respondents answered this way.

✛ Only 13 percent of adults said that, as a child or teenager, they had an alcohol or drug use problem. The figure for trans persons was more than double, 29 percent.

✛ When asked about depression and anxiety, 32 percent of adults said they had such problems growing up. For trans adults the number was an astonishing 78 percent.

[195] Michael W. Chapman, "Johns Hopkins Psychiatrist: Transgender Is 'Mental Disorder'; Sex Change 'Biologically Impossible,'" CNS News, November 26, 2020, https://www.cnsnews.com/article/national/michael-w-chapman/johns-hopkins-psychiatrist-transgender-mental-disorder-sex/.

[196] Bill Donohue, "Trans Persons Admit to Mental Disorders," Catholic League, May 8, 2023, https://www.catholicleague.org/trans-persons-admit-to-mental-disorders/.

Respondents were asked how often they felt in the past twelve months about several emotional conditions:

✣ Lonely: 21 percent of adults answered always/often; 45 percent of trans persons answered this way.

✣ Hopeful: 50 percent of adults reported always/often, but only 29 percent of trans adults felt this way.

✣ Depressed: 22 percent of adults admitted to depression, but almost half, 48 percent of trans persons, confessed to being depressed.

✣ Anxious: The figure for adults was 31 percent; for trans persons, it was 56 percent.

✣ Happy: 59 percent of adults said they were happy, but only 40 percent of trans persons said they were.

When trans persons were asked about abnormal behaviors, the results were predictable.

✣ Engaged in self-harm: For adults, the number was 3 percent; it was 17 percent for trans adults.

✣ Suicidal thoughts: 16 percent of adults, and 43 percent of trans respondents, said they thought about killing themselves.

The conventional wisdom, as entertained by elites, is that any mental health problems that trans persons have is a result of discrimination. But that is not what the survey suggests.

✤ When those who identify as trans were asked
  if they had ever been refused health care from
  a health care provider, or someone else working in a health care setting, 82 percent said
  "no."

✤ When asked if they had been denied a job or
  promotion, 78 percent said they had not.

✤ When asked if they had ever been evicted or
  denied housing, 86 percent said "no."

It is not societal rejection of trans males and females that is the
root of their problem. Their problem lies deep within themselves. They are unhappy, lonely, depressed persons who are
more likely to engage in self-destructive behaviors. That's not
normal. It's sad. But their sexually confused status is a symptom
of underlying mental health problems—and they need help.

No mental health problem is more serious than contem-
plating suicide. A survey by the Williams Institute reported
that 41 percent of trans adults have attempted suicide, compared to 4.6 percent in the general population.[197] Moreover,
studies have shown that the suicide rate spikes ten to fifteen
years post-surgery; this is twenty times higher than in the
non-trans population.[198]

[197] J. Michael Bailey and Ray Blanchard, "Suicide or Transition: The
  Only Options for Gender Dysphoric Kids?," 4thWaveNow, September 8, 2017, https://4thwavenow.com/2017/09.08/suicide-
  or-transition-the-only-options-for-gender-dysphoric-kids/.

[198] Alicia Ault, "Doctors Have Failed Them, Say Those Who
  Regret Transitioning," WebMD, March 22, 2022, https://
  www.webmd.com/sex-relationships/news/2022/03/22/
  doctors-have-failed-them-say-those-who-regret-transitioning/.

Dr. Michael Bailey and Dr. Ray Blanchard are two psychology professors who are very familiar with the mental health challenges that transgender people face. But some of their findings run counter to the received wisdom: "There is no persuasive evidence that gender transition reduced gender dysphoric children's likelihood of killing themselves. The idea that mental health problems — including suicidality — are caused by gender dysphoria rather than the other way around ... is currently popular and politically correct. It is, however, unproven and as likely to be false as true."[199]

Dr. Paul Sullins, a Catholic priest and sociology professor, sums up the issue well. "If we demand that a cause must precede an effect," he wryly notes, "then the higher rate of suicide attempts among sexual minorities (over four times that of heterosexual persons) is more likely related to the higher rate of childhood sexual abuse they experience (also four times that of heterosexual persons) than to persistent social discrimination."[200]

Trans activists ignore the data. They are convinced that the mental health issues that trans persons experience are a result of the way they are treated. Worse, they, and many therapists, try to convince parents that if they do not affirm their child's decision to transition, their child is likely to commit suicide.

[199] Bailey and Blanchard, "Suicide or Transition."
[200] "Catholic University of America Professor Pushes Back against 'Reparative Therapy' Studies," *National Catholic Register*, March 27, 2023, https://www.ncregister.com/interview/catholic-university-of-america-professor-pushes-back-against-reparative-theapy-studies/.

This situation is so perverse that there are even those who laud the suicide of trans youth, saying it is a sign of bravery. In 2014, Leelah Alcorn killed herself, and in 2022, Dr. Morissa Ladinsky, a professor of pediatrics, stunned thousands of her colleagues at the American Academy of Pediatrics' annual conference when she eulogized the teenager. She heralded her for "step[ing] boldly in front of a tractor trailer, ending her life." One of the pediatricians, Dr. Julia Mason, who witnessed her talk, accused her of "glorifying suicide," saying it was "unprofessional and dangerous."[201]

In her book on transgenderism, Abigail Shrier said the gambit of frightening parents of trans children who want to transition is commonplace. "It's a gun to the head: do as your kid says, or she just might take her own life. Again and again, I heard this question from gender therapists and also from parents to whom they had spoken: '*Would you rather a dead daughter or a live son?*'"[202] According to one trans youth Shrier interviewed, "It's essentially emotional blackmail."[203]

No wonder Dr. Michelle Cretella, executive director of the American College of Pediatricians, says that some gender experts are so far gone that they will "seek to involve child protective services against transgender-hesitant parents based

---

[201] Aaron Sibarium, "Pediatric Group Says Kids Should Talk to Their Parents about Tattoos—but Not Puberty Blockers," *New York Post*, December 7, 2022, https://nypost.com/2022/12/07/pediatric-group-says-kids-should-not-talk-to-parents-about-puberty-blockers/.

[202] Shrier, *Irreversible Damage*, 107.

[203] Ibid., 138.

on the lie that children will commit suicide without trans-affirmative counseling and transgender drugs."[204]

VIOLENT TENDENCIES

It is one thing to be unhappy, quite another to be angry. Regrettably, many trans persons are very angry, and their anger is directed at those they like to call "cisgender" persons, which is everyone who is not in rebellion against his or her nature-based sex—in other words, most of the world.

Brown University professor Lisa Littman found how deep the anger runs. Trans persons like to mock heterosexuals and so-called cisgender persons. They particularly loathe white males. Some say they are evil; others simply find them "privileged, dumb and boring." Marriage is often spoken about with derision, as is the nuclear family. It is not uncommon for trans youth to turn on their parents, even to the point of calling their mothers "breeders." "If they aren't mocking 'cis' people," one parent told Littman, "they are playing pronoun police and mocking people who can't get the pronouns correct." Others gleefully see themselves as victims, perceiving it "as a badge of honor."[205]

Just as it is possible to be unhappy without being angry, it is possible to be angry without being violent. But in the case of trans persons, too often their anger takes a violent turn.

[204] Stephen M. Krason, ed., *Parental Rights in Peril* (Steubenville, OH: Franciscan University Press, 2022), 114.
[205] Littman, "Parent Reports."

A 2022 Canadian study found trans youth are at the highest risk of "violent radicalization." The research was extensive, covering eighteen different colleges in Quebec. Of the thirty-one hundred participants between the ages of sixteen and twenty-five years old, 2.5 percent were trans. It found that "transgender and gender diverse students reported higher support for VR [violent radicalization] compared to students who identified as women."[206]

In March 2023, there were four instances of pro-trans protesters occupying state capitols in one week. There were also four mass shootings committed by trans persons in the previous five years.

In one instance, Audrey Hale, a female who identified as male, killed six innocent people in Nashville, Tennessee. The local police said she was planning the attack "over a period of months," and that she had studied other mass murderers. Importantly, they found a manifesto that laid bare her thinking. Her "calculated and planned" attack was directed at a Christian school, Covenant, and the affiliated Covenant church she had once attended. "There's some belief that there was some resentment for having to go to that school," said Police Chief John Drake.[207] As expected, the media downplayed the identity of the mass shooter, and they

---

[206] Spencer Lindquist, "Study: 'Transgender' Youth at Highest Risk for Violent Radicalization," Breitbart, March 28, 2023, https://breitbart.com/politics/study-transgender-youth-at-highest-risk-for-violent-radicalization/.

[207] Bill Donohue, "Where Is the Nashville Manifesto?," Catholic League, April 24, 2023, https://www.catholicleague.org/where-is-the-nashville-manifesto/.

certainly made no effort to have her manifesto released. The thought of outing a trans killer who hated Christianity was enough to bury the story.

Radicals who support the trans agenda are not reluctant to use violence to achieve their ends. Antifa, an urban terrorist group, is quick to engage in violence whenever there is a protest against a drag queen event.

In 2022, Antifa members came armed with AR-15 rifles and handguns to what was billed as a "kid-friendly" drag show in Roanoke, Texas; they said they showed up to protect the show. They did the same in Fort Worth, Texas, in 2023. As noted by journalist Andy Ngo, Antifa is more than an advocate for transgenderism. "In my reporting on Antifa for years now, one observation that I noticed was that disproportionately, the number of riot arrestees are gender diverse. And by that, I mean, they don't identify with their biological sex. In some nights, it was as high as 20 percent, and that is magnitudes higher than what the data we have on people in the wider American population who are trans identifying."[208]

Trans activists and their supporters also like to highlight violence against trans persons themselves. President Biden decries it, as does the National Education Association — and they are right to call attention to it. But what they don't mention is that the people who are committing violence are often trans people themselves.

[208] Ngo made his comments on *Tucker Carlson Tonight*, aired March 28, 2023, on Fox News.

Psycom Pro is a psychiatry resource for clinicians, and in 2022 it concluded that "more than half of transgender individuals experience partner violence or gender identity abuse."[209]

In 2020, seven experts published a study in the *American Journal of Public Health* on "intimate partner violence" among trans persons. They concluded that "transgender individuals experience a dramatically higher prevalence of IPV [intimate partner violence] victimization compared with cisgender individuals, regardless of sex assigned at birth."

The National Coalition Against Domestic Violence reviewed the literature on domestic violence in the LGBT community and found that "43.8% of lesbian women and 61.1% of bisexual women have experienced rape, physical violence, and/or stalking by an intimate partner at some point in their lifetime, as opposed to 35% of cisgender women." It also found that "transgender individuals suffer from an even greater burden of intimate partner violence than gay or lesbian individuals."[210]

The Williams Institute, a think tank at UCLA Law, reviewed a number of studies on this subject. One of them found that "31.1% of transgender people and 20.4% of cisgender people had ever experienced IPV or dating violence." It also said that three studies concluded that the

---

[209] Bill Donohue, "Dirty Little Secret about Trans Violence," Catholic League, May 18, 2023, https://www.catholicleague. org/dirty-little-secret-about-trans-violence-2/.

[210] Ibid.

lifetime intimate partner sexual violence prevalence among transgender people ranged from "20.0% to 47.0%."

Even in sympathetic pop culture magazines, such as *Portland Monthly*, it is acknowledged that "statistically speaking, the most common perpetrators of violence against trans women are domestic partners."[211]

Virtually every study has concluded that trans people suffer from high rates of depression, anxiety, suicidal ideation, and suicide, making it plain that this is a population plagued by mental illnesses. How much this contributes to their propensity for violence is not known. But we know one thing for sure: it is not white heterosexual Christian men who are roaming the streets looking for trans people to beat up—it is trans people who are committing the violence.

What's Driving Transgenderism

The good news is that in recent years there has been more and more pushback against a rash of transitioning. But the pushback is not coming from elite quarters; it is coming from ordinary Americans.

A poll conducted by Scott Rasmussen in 2022 found that 72 percent of people surveyed oppose schools teaching children they can change their sex; 80 percent said that parents should be given advance notice of any such instruction. Even 60 percent consider school programs that encourage

[211] Ibid.

transitioning to be engaging in child abuse.[212] A Rasmussen survey in 2023 revealed that 58 percent of Americans at least somewhat approve of "legislation making it illegal to perform sex-change surgery on minors," including 46 percent who "strongly approve" of such laws.[213]

A poll by McLaughlin & Associates in 2023 found that 71 percent of voters are angry and upset by drag queen shows, school curricula, and social media, all of which function to encourage kids to transition.[214] A year earlier, this polling company reported that 75 percent of voters who had an opinion on transgenderism felt the movement "had gone too far" by encouraging minors to transition.[215]

Moreover, as Kara Dansky disclosed, "increasing numbers of lesbians, gay men, and bisexual people (LGB) are taking a stand against the inclusion of 'T' in the acronym

[212] Jazz Shaw, "Strong Majority of Americans See Elements of Trans Agenda as Child Abuse," *Hot Air*, October 31, 2022, http://hotair.com/jazz-shaw/2022/10/31/strong-majority-of-americans-see-elements-of-trans-agenda-as-child-abuse-n506884/.

[213] Ryan Foley, "Most Americans Support State Laws Banning Sex Change Surgeries for Minors, Poll Finds," *Christian Post*, February 20, 2023, https://www.christianpost.com/news/most-favor-banning-surgeries-for-kids-poll.html/.

[214] Tyler O'Neil, "'The Transgender Movement Is Actually an Industry' by Which Big Pharma Earns 'Obscene Profits,' Authors Warn," Daily Signal, March 9, 2023. https://www.dailysignal.com//print?post_id=974417/.

[215] Christina Buttons, "Poll: Majority Of American Voters Say Transgender Movement's Targeting of Underage Minors Has Gone Too Far," *Daily Wire*, October 29, 2022, https://www.dailywire.com/news/poll/-majority-of-american-voters-say-transgender-movements-targeting-of-underage-minors-has-gone-too-far/.

LGBT because sexual orientation and 'gender identity' have nothing to do with each other, although they are typically linked together."[216]

So who are the most likely to support transgenderism? Well-educated, wealthy white secularists. Blacks are the least likely.

In 2023, the Pew Research Center published a survey that found that among whites, only 27 percent believe that our sex is determined at birth; 72 percent said it can be different. Among blacks, 66 percent answered correctly, that is, our sex is known at birth; 33 percent said it can change.[217] Why are whites so gullible and obtuse? The answer is obvious: there is nothing about race that makes someone smart. But there is something about the college experience—and whites are much more likely to go to college—that impairs the ability to think independently. Quite frankly, many students have been intellectually abused by their professors.

White college-educated female Democrats are the most likely to believe the fiction that men can become pregnant, with 36 percent answering affirmatively.[218] Who are the most likely to believe the lie that it is possible to change our

---

[216] Danksy, *The Abolition of Sex*, 8.
[217] John Gramlich, "Black Democrats Differ from Other Democrats in Their Views on Gender Identity, Transgender Issues," Pew Research Center, January 4, 2023, https://www.pewresearch.org/fact-tank/2023/01/04/black-democrats-differ-from-other-democrats-in-their-views-on-gender-identity-transgender-issues/.
[218] Bill Donohue, "Why Are College Grads So Superstitious?," Catholic League, September 12, 2022, https://www.catholicleague.org/why-are-college-grads-so-superstitious?/.

sex? Those with a college education or more. In 2021, Pew found that those who are the most likely to believe that we can change our sex are liberal Democrats; 81 percent believe this to be true.[219] (Remember, we know from an earlier Pew survey that those with a college education are also less religious than other Americans.[220])

These data take on great significance when we learn which parents of trans youth are the biggest problem. Professor Lisa Littman found that they are overwhelmingly white, well-educated, and politically very liberal. Naturally, they support gay and transgender rights.[221] This makes perfect sense. These persons are, again, the most secular segment of the population. Moreover, they have all the earmarks of the effects of higher education. It is not the daughters of cops and the sons of firefighters who are transitioning—it's the children of those who have been propagandized by college and post-graduate education.

One of the most disgraceful aspects of transgenderism is the push by some therapists, activists, parents, and teachers to enable, if not encourage, sexually confused young people to transition. If they just backed off—or better yet, counseled confused children to wait it out—80 percent of young

[219] Bill Donohue, "Why Are Educated White People So Stupid?," Catholic League, July 28, 2021, https://www.catholicleague.org/why-are-educated-white-people-so-stupid?/.

[220] "In America, Does More Education Equal Less Religion?," Pew Research Center, April 26, 2017, https://www.pewresearch.org/religion/2017/04/26/in-america-does-more-education-equal-less-religion/.

[221] Littman, "Parent Reports."

people will grow out of their confusion. This is true in the United States and Europe.

Regrettably, powerful ideological and financial incentives work to encourage transition. This includes Disney. Not only do Disney movies, aimed at children, now regularly feature trans characters, but the elites who run the once family-friendly empire have pledged to include many more. For example, in its *Baymax!* series, Disney showed a man buying tampons; this was done intentionally to promote transgenderism and confuse young people about their own gender. As I said in an award-winning documentary the Catholic League did on Disney, "Walt Disney must be turning over in his grave."

One of the most important forces aiding and abetting this craze is social media, and no one is more susceptible to the influence of social media than girls. They are the biggest users of social media—and girls are three times more likely to want to transition to the opposite sex than boys. (Before the rise of social media, boys were more likely to want to transition.)

In her groundbreaking book on transgenderism, Abigail Shrier found that for "nearly all of the parents I spoke to, their daughters' announcement on social media of a transgender identity was a turning point. From then on, everyone knew. From then on—and sometimes despite their daughters' lingering doubts—their daughters felt locked in. It became a choice they couldn't easily take back."[222]

[222] Shrier, *Irreversible Damage*, 214.

Even Marci Bowers, president of the World Professional Association for Transgender Health, admits that "social contagion," or what she prefers to call "peer influence," is real, though "people in my community," she says, deny its existence.[223] Jonathan Haidt, a well-respected psychologist, says we are facing a "mental health crisis," attributable, he contends, to social media.[224] Tumblr, Instagram, TikTok, and YouTube have played a critical role in driving this disaster.

Helena Kerschner, a young girl who detransitioned, explained what happened to her: "My dysphoria was definitely triggered by this online community. I never thought about my gender or had a problem with being a girl before going on Tumblr."[225]

Littman found conclusive evidence of the effects of social media on young people considering a transition to the other sex. She pioneered the "social contagion" theory in her 2018 peer-reviewed paper when she coined the term *rapid-onset gender dysphoria*, meaning the sudden and surprisingly emergence of a conflict between a person's birth sex and their sex identity.[226] But her critics did not want to

---

[223] Rich Lowry, "Social Contagion Is Making Teen Girls Depressed — and Trans," *New York Post*, March 28, 2023, https://nypost.com/2023/03/27/social-contagion-is-making-teen-girls-depressed-and-trans/.

[224] Shrier, *Irreversible Damage*, 3.

[225] Rikki Schlott, "'I Literally Lost Organs': Why Detransitioned Teens Regret Changing Genders," *New York Post*, June 18, 2022, https://nypost.com/2022/06/18/detransitioned-teens-explain-why-they-regret-changing-genders/.

[226] Littman, "Parent Reports."

admit the obvious: that the dramatic explosion in trans youth is a culturally produced phenomenon. Because she challenged the conventional thinking, she was condemned by academicians and activists. Brown University even pulled its promotion of her work.[227] In short, the Left tried to silence her.

The fact is, parents of trans youth agree that rapid-onset gender dysphoria is a reality. A survey of these parents found that the majority said they felt pressure from a "gender clinic or specialist" to transition their child socially or medically. When the parents were asked if the friends of their trans child "came out as transgender around the same time," most answered affirmatively, thus supporting social contagion theory. A majority of parents also confessed that their gender-dysphoric child had preexisting mental health issues.[228] No wonder the number of prescriptions for puberty blockers for those under the age of eighteen doubled between 2017 and 2021.[229]

[227] Bill Donohue, "Left-Wing Reaction to Trans Killer Is Typical," Catholic League, March 30, 2023, https://catholicleague.org/left-wing-reaction-to-trans-killer-is-typical/.

[228] Wesley J. Smith, "Parents' Survey of Rapid-Onset Gender Dysphoric Kids Finds Preexisting Mental-Health Issues and Pressured Parents," *National Review*, April 3, 2023, https://www.nationalreview.com/corner/parents-survey-of-rapid-onset-gender-dysphoric-kids-finds-preexisting-mental-health-issues-and-pressured-parents/.

[229] Mary Harrington, "American Kids Are in the Grip of a Gender Contagion," *New York Post*, December 21, 2022, https://nypost.com/2022/12/20/american-kids-are-in-the-grip-of-a-gender-contagion/.

THE ROLE OF THE MEDICAL PROFESSION

The medical profession has suffered a loss of prestige in recent years. The inconsistent, and at times incoherent, response to COVID played a role. But a more serious problem has been its response to transgenderism.

There's big money in transitioning; it's a multibillion-dollar enterprise.[230] Offering its support to this exploitative campaign is the World Health Organization, which boasts of its updated manual on gender mainstreaming for health managers. The new features go "beyond non-binary approaches to gender and health to recognize gender and sexual diversity, or the concepts that gender identity exists on a continuum and that sex is not limited to male and female."[231] They did not give a name to the third sex.

Boston was the epicenter of the clergy sexual abuse scandal in the Catholic Church, which was properly condemned. Now it is the epicenter of child abuse again—but this time it is the medical profession that is the culprit. Few elites are objecting; most are in favor of it, and those who condemn it are themselves condemned.

Gender Multispecialty Service is part of Boston Children's Hospital. The unit is known as one of the most advanced and prominent institutions of its kind in the

---

[230] Tyler O'Neil, "New Book Follows Money Trail behind 'Insane' Lie That 'Splits Families' and Causes 'Permanent Medical Damage,' Authors Say," Daily Signal, March 9, 2023, https://www.dailysignal.com/.

[231] Bill Donohue, "The Gall of World Health Officials," Catholic League, September 19, 2022, https://www.catholicleague.org/the-gall-of-world-health-officials-2/.

nation that provides sex-reassignment operations on children. Kerry McGregor, a psychologist who works there, claims that "a good portion of children do know as early as, seemingly from the womb," what their sex is.[232] She did not say how she knows this—the kids cannot yet talk—but somehow she does.

McGregor also says some children choose their sex "as soon as they can talk." How does that work? "They might say phrases, such as 'I'm a girl' or 'I'm a boy' or 'I'm going to be a woman' or 'I'm going to be a mom.' Kids know very, very early."[233]

No they don't. This is nonsense. When over eleven thousand parents were asked in 2021 what their baby's first words were, the top three were "Dad (or Dada, Daddy, Papa, etc.); Mom (or Mama, Mommy, Mum, etc.); and Hi (or Hiya, Hey, Heya, Hello)." In the top fifteen choices, none mentioned anything remotely about being a boy or a girl.[234]

It's not just a few activists who have infiltrated the medical industry—the American Medical Association (AMA) itself is on board too: "Designating sex on birth certificates as male or female, and making that information available on the public portion, perpetuates a view that sex designation is permanent and fails to recognize the medical spectrum of

[232] Bill Donohue, "Beware of Transgender Psychologists," Catholic League, August 16, 2022, https://www.catholicleague.org/beware-of-transgender-psychologists/.
[233] Ibid.
[234] Ibid.

gender identity."[235] Once again, subjective interpretations of one's sex that are untethered from reality are now being treated as if they were true.

The American Academy of Pediatrics not only agrees with the AMA, but it also forbids doctors who are comfortable telling the truth from setting up booths at its annual conferences and from challenging its flawed transgender position.[236] The transgender movement is also supported by the Federation of Pediatric Organizations, which is comprised of seven of the most prominent pediatric associations in the United States.[237] The American Psychological Association[238] and the American Psychiatric Association[239] have also bought into it.

In 2023, the American Academy of Pediatrics reaffirmed its child gender transition policy, giving the green light to procedures that include genital mutilation and chemical castration. In doing so, it was not only going against public opinion, but it was going against the conventional thinking of the medical establishment in Europe. Dr. Stanley Goldfarb, chairman of the medical advocacy group Do No Harm,

[235] Bill Donohue, "Transgender Reports Are Startling," Catholic League, August 23, 2021, https//www.catholicleague.org/transgender-reports-are-startling/.

[236] Ibid.

[237] "Statement Published in Support of Transgender Children and Youth, Their Families, and Health Care Providers," American Board of Pediatrics, March 28, 2022, abp.org/news/press-releases-statement-published-support-transgender-children-and-youth-their-families-and-health-care-providers/.

[238] Schlott, "I Literally Lost Organs."

[239] Krason, *Parental Rights in Peril*, 112–113.

blasted this decision: "In the face of increasing evidence that so-called gender-affirming care does more harm than good in the opinion of the leaders of the field of gender medicine in Norway, Finland, Sweden, and the United Kingdom, the American Academy of Pediatrics is doubling down in support of the current approach."[240]

The elites who treat our mental and physical health have become full-time advocates of transgenderism. Quite frankly, the medical profession probably knows better. In fact, the Catholic League did a study of two of the most widely used textbooks by medical students in the United States: Anne M. Gilroy's *Anatomy: An Essential Textbook*, third edition, published by Thieme Medical Publishers; and *Gray's Anatomy for Students* fourth edition, written by Richard L. Drake, A. Wayne Vogl, and Adam W. M. Mitchell, published by Elsevier. Both books contained references to male and female, but none for transgender, intersex, or "other sexes or genders."[241]

The fact is, no transgender gene has ever been found. Moreover, there are an estimated sixty-five hundred biological differences between males and females.[242] Like it or not, these are hard scientific facts that cannot be ignored.

[240] Breccan F. Thies, "U.S. Pediatricians 'Reaffirm' Child Gender Transition Policy as Europe Sounds Alarm," *Washington Examiner*, August 12, 2023.

[241] Bill Donohue, "Anatomy Texts Prove Women Exist," Catholic League, May 2, 2022, https://www.catholicleague.org/anatomy-texts-prove-women-exist/.

[242] O'Neil, "'Transgender Movement."

Dr. Christiane Nüsslein-Volhard is a Nobel Prize–winning developmental biologist. She calls the transgender movement's claims "unscientific" and "nonsense," and says that allowing teenagers to determine their own sex is "madness." Furthermore, she says, "All mammals have two sexes, and man is a mammal. There's the one sex that produces the eggs, has two X chromosomes. That's called female. And there's the other one that makes the sperm, has an X and a Y chromosome. That's called male."[243]

Unfortunately, the medical establishment has decided that playing politics is more important than protecting health. Fortunately, the public is onto them, which is why the reputation of the medical establishment has taken such a hit. If they want to recover it, the prescription is to get back to basics and to start being doctors again — and to kick the unhealthy habit of indulging in political madness.

The Role of Schools

Schools are one of the biggest drivers of transgenderism. While much of the pro-trans movement is confined to public schools, there are plenty of private schools — especially the most expensive and prominent ones — that have jumped on the trans bandwagon.

[243] Gary Benoit, "Nobel Prize–Winning German Biologist: Multiple Genders Are 'Nonsense' and 'Unscientific,'" *The New American*, August 29, 2022, https://thenewamerican.com/nobel-prize-winning-german-biologist-multiple-genders-are-nonsense-and-unscientific/.

One thing that virtually all of these schools have in common is a general loathing of parental rights. The degree of dishonesty—of out-and-out lying to parents—is astonishing. Many administrators and teachers really believe they have every right to make decisions for children that have always been reserved for parents.

This is another manifestation of the religious-secular divide. Aquinas was so insistent that children belong to parents that he opposed Christians baptizing Jews, even when that view was controversial. He warned Christians that they had no business making such a decision, even if it was done with the intent of saving someone's soul, because children belong by nature to their parents. By contrast, secular-minded administrators believe their progressive programs are good for children—so parents' rights be damned.

In 2023, Kathy McCord was fired as a student counselor from an Indiana high school for openly condemning a secret transgender policy that kept parents in the dark about their children's "gender transitions." The vote by the school board to oust her, after twenty-five years of service, was unanimous.[244] This kind of ruling is not an anomaly. The National Education Association is on record saying that when a trans student publicly shares his or her new identity, "the parents should *not* be informed."[245] The hijacking of parental rights

[244] Tony Kinnett, "Indiana Student Counselor Fired for Condemning School District's Hidden Transgender Policy," Daily Signal, March 9, 2023, https://www.dailysignal.com/.
[245] Shrier, *Irreversible Damage*, 74.

is also supported by many in the media. Sarah Jones wrote a piece for *New York Magazine* arguing that parents have no right to claim their children as "private property"—they are a public responsibility, she said.[246]

Some schools, such as one in Colorado, actually employ LGBT activists to train school nurses to ask students what pronoun they like when called on in class. "Transgender and non-binary students have the right to discuss and express their gender identity and expression openly and to decide which, with whom, and how much to share their private information," the training stated.[247]

In 2023, the Catholic League released a report, "Sexualizing Children in the Schools," that detailed just how morally debased this kind of instruction is. For example, middle school children in Massachusetts are being told how to use cling wrap as a dental dam around their teeth for safe oral sex. High school students in California are given school books containing graphic sexual imagery and information about orgies, sex parties, and BDSM. Spring Lake Public Schools in Michigan offered the book *Gender Queer* in school libraries. The book is a graphic novel memoir and features mature sexual content and images of

[246] Sarah Jones, "Children Are Not Property," *New York Magazine*, April 8, 2023, www.nymag.com/intelligencer/2023/04/children-are-not-property.html/.

[247] Reagan Reese, "School District's LGBTQ Coordinator Trained Nurses to Hide Student's Gender Transitions," *Daily Caller*, May 3, 2023, https://www.dailycaller.com/.

nude individuals engaging in sex acts.[248] These educators are odious and malicious.

Indeed, it is truly hard to believe what is actually happening in some of these schools. Travis Allen is a girls' soccer coach at a public school in Vermont. He was suspended from his job without pay because he complained about a male student roaming around the girls' locker room. His daughter, who is on the volleyball team, also spoke out about this incident. She saw the male student in the locker room and publicly stated how uncomfortable she was with this situation; she and the boy were both fourteen. But she was the one suspended for complaining. (The school dropped the suspension after her parents filed a lawsuit.[249])

It's not just in schools where this is happening. A teenage girl in California was showering at a YMCA when a naked man entered the locker room. She complained. The YMCA did nothing about it. As long as he was not on a sex offender registry, she was told, grown men can shower alongside teenage girls.[250]

It's amazing. And sick. Schools can't give aspirin or Benadryl to students without parental consent. But they can give them contraceptives and advice on how to change their sex—behind the backs of their parents. A dean at an elite private school in Chicago bragged how during Pride Week,

---

[248] Bill Donohue, "Sexualizing Children in the Schools," Catholic League, May 31, 2023, https://www.catholicleague.org/sexualizing-children-in-the-schools/.

[249] Allen's remarks were made on *Tucker Carlson Tonight*, aired October 27, 2022, on Fox News.

[250] See *Tucker Carlson Tonight*, Fox News, January 17, 2023.

LGBT activists were allowed to share sex toys with students, as well as devices that would make most parents vomit.[251] When a seventh-grade boy masturbated in front of class-mates in a California school, the superintendent defended him, saying what he did was normal.[252] A gay male teacher came to class in Seattle wearing a skirt, and with the intent of explaining to his preschool students that it was totally okay for men to dress this way.[253]

Madness. And if parents don't object — vigorously and continuously until it stops — it is bound to continue. Parents are the only ones who can turn things around.

THE ROLE OF GOVERNMENT

The transgender movement could not have succeeded without the help of government. The government's involvement really began in 2014 when the Obama administration overturned a rule that barred the use of Medicare funds to pay for

[251] "Elite Chicago Private School's Dean of Students Brags about Bringing in LGBTQ+ Health Center to Teach 'Queer Sex' to Minors," Project Veritas, December 7, 2022, https://www.projectveritas.com/news/elite-chicago-private-schools-dean-of-students-brags-about-bringing-in-lgbtq/.

[252] Corrine Murdock, "Southern California Superintendent Defends Seventh-Grade Boy Masturbating in Front of Classmates, Claims It's Normal," *Daily Wire*, October 12, 2022, https://www.dailywire.com/news/southern-california-superintendent-defends-7th-grade-boy-masturbating-in-front-of-classmates-claims-its-normal/.

[253] "Preschool Teachers Drill Students in 'Woke' Gender Language," Free Beacon, February 15, 2023, https://freebeacon.com/campus/watch-preschool-teachers-drill-students-in-woke-gender-language/.

transitioning from one sex to another. Two years later, the Affordable Care Act, or Obamacare, forced health care providers and insurers to pay for sex-change operations. This resulted in a massive increase in sex-reassignment surgeries: they jumped from 3,256 in 2016 to 8,304 in 2017, the largest single-year spike of 155 percent ever recorded.

If Obama opened the door to funding sex-change procedures, it was left to the Biden administration to promulgate a far more aggressive pro-transgender policy. On March 31, 2022, "Transgender Day of Visibility," President Biden took the opportunity to commend the parents of transgender children for "affirming your child's identity," saying it is "one of the most powerful things you can do to keep them safe and healthy."[254] This is the mindset of the president and an administration that purports to be compassionate but in reality is promoting child abuse on a massive scale.

Given this ideological framework, it was not surprising to learn that when Florida barred hormone therapy, sex-change operations, and other irreversible surgeries on children, Biden said this was "close to sinful."[255] One wonders if he really knows the mental and physical damage that

[254] Bill Donohue, "Biden Is Clueless on Transgender Youth," Catholic League, April 11, 2022, https://www.catholicleague.org/biden-is-clueless-on-transgender-youth/.

[255] David Ng, "Joe Biden Calls Florida Barring Transgender Procedures on Children 'Close to Sinful' in 'Daily Show' Interview," Breitbart, March 13, 2023, https://www.breitbart.com/entertainment/2023/03/13/joe-biden-calls-florida-barring-transgender-procedures-on-children-close-to-sinful-in-daily-show-interview/.

these transgender procedures do to children. If he doesn't, he is shamefully ignorant. If he does, he is evil.

Biden wasted no time championing the transgender cause. He appointed a man who had transitioned to "be" a woman (or so he said) as his new assistant health secretary. When "Rachel" Levine was asked by a lawyer for the Trump administration, "What does it mean to be a male or female?" the good doctor could not answer.[256] Similarly, when Supreme Court nominee Ketanji Brown Jackson was asked what a woman is, she could not provide an answer; she was confirmed anyway.[257] When Biden's secretary of health and human services, Xavier Becerra, was asked why the administration doesn't refer to those who give birth as women, rather as "birthing people," he said, "I'll have to check the language there, but I think if we're talking about those who give birth, I think we're talking about—I don't know how else to explain it."[258] In 2023, the Biden administration gave an "International Women of Courage Award" to Alba Rueda, a man who identifies as a woman.[259] But Joe Biden regularly assures us he is Mr. Devout Catholic.

[256] Bill Donohue, "Sex Transitioning for Minors Is Child Abuse," Catholic League, March 29, 2021, https://www.catholicleague.org/sex-transitioning-for-minors-is-child-abuse/.

[257] Kate Scanlon, "Jackson Says She Cannot Define What a Woman Is at Confirmation," *Washington Examiner*, March 22, 2022.

[258] Elizabeth Troutman, "Biden Is Confused about Who Can Get Pregnant, Women's History Month Proclamation Shows," Daily Signal, March 1, 2023, https://www.dailysignal.com.

[259] Leif Le Mahieu, "Biden Admin Gives 'International Women of Courage Award' to a Biological Man," *Daily Wire*, March 8, 2023, https://www.dailywire.com/news/biden-admin-gives-international-women-of-courage-award-to-a-biological-man/.

Where will all of this wind up? There are signs that resistance to the transgender movement is gaining ground. There will doubtless be more lawsuits against the trans industry, and that will certainly help. But at its root, this is a moral crisis, a reflection of our cultural meltdown. The elite ruling class created this insanity, by promoting a secular vision of man and society—but we have allowed this secular vision to prevail. Things will only change when there is enough pushback from below.

Meanwhile, the child abuse will continue.

PART III

SECULAR SUICIDE

CHAPTER 5

DIVIDED WE FALL

PATRIOTISM MATTERS

MANY OF THE PUBLIC policies that have created serious social problems are the result of good intentions gone awry. But some are the result of policies that were never directed toward achieving the common good: they are the result of decisions aimed at advancing a political agenda, rather than the best interests of society.

"United we stand, divided we fall" is a phrase traceable to the sixth-century B.C. Greek storyteller Aesop. It is the message of his fable "The Four Oxen and the Lion," in which four oxen survived against a lion as long as they stood back to back but, when they began to bicker and separated, were each devoured in turn. Jesus made a similar statement, one that has more currency for Americans today: "Every kingdom divided against itself will be laid waste, and no town or house divided against itself will stand" (Matt. 12:25). More recently, Cardinal Robert Sarah has noted, "The sign of Satan is division."[260]

This accurately describes the polarization that is abundantly evident in society today. It also reflects the clash between a religious vision of morality and a secular one. As we saw in the last two chapters, these two visions have wildly different notions of liberty. In this chapter, we will explore their dramatically different notions of equality.

The religious vision understands that every man and woman is made in God's image and likeness, and that each possesses equal dignity, independent of social characteristics. We are called to work for the common good, and to bring people together. This certainly means treating everyone as an equal. But it does not mean that all existing inequalities are morally problematic. There is a difference between inequalities that develop as a result of different individual faculties, and inequalities that develop as a result of unfair treatment. We should all labor to promote justice. But it behooves us to acknowledge that, given the reality of sin, this labor is, and always will be, a never-ending effort.

The secular vision sees inequality as inherently unjust, even immoral, and therefore deserving of eradication. It discounts differences in talent and ambition, and focuses on socially contrived mechanisms that generate group inequalities. Most important, because it does not recognize the natural limits of the human condition, it believes that human perfectibility is possible. Unavoidably, the gap between the ideal and

---

[260] Robert Cardinal Sarah, *The Day Is Now Far Spent* (San Francisco: Ignatius Press, 2021), 134–135.

the real becomes cause for discontent, and even anger. This anger often manifests itself in socially divisive ways and treats appeals to the common good as sophistry.

The differences between these two visions of man and society are stark and irreconcilable. In short, the religious vision is realistic, and tempered by man's sinful nature. The secular vision is utopian, and not tempered by anything. The elites in our society incline toward the secular vision. They are thus largely responsible for the social turmoil that exists.

Aquinas understood that man is "a social and political animal" that needs to check his self-interest for the common good. In every society, he said, there must be "some governing power" to direct people toward the "common good." "The common good" is one of the four pillars of Catholic social teaching, the others being the "dignity of the person," "subsidiarity," and "solidarity."[261] All of these aspects of Catholic social thought are predicated on the need for social cohesion, a condition that is increasingly elusive.

Our lack of cohesion is manifested in many ways, one of which is the declining sense of patriotism. Aquinas maintained that reverence toward country "includes homage to all our fellow-citizens and to all the friends of our country."[262] The good news is that most Americans want a united country

---

[261] Michael P. Orsi, "Catholic Social Thought," in *Encyclopedia of Catholic Social Thought, Social Science, and Social Policy*, ed. Michael Coulter, Stephen Krason, Richard Myers, and Joseph Varacalli (Lanham, MD: Scarecrow Press, Inc., 2007), 152–153.

[262] C. C. Pecknold, "What St. Thomas Aquinas Teaches Us about Patriotism," *Catholic Herald*, July 4, 2019, https://catholicherald.co.uk/what-st-thomas-aquinas-teaches-us-about-patriotism/.

and are proud of their history. But there is a determined and well-organized effort on the part of left-wing activists to undermine those sentiments. This effort is rooted in a contempt for our religious heritage.

Steve Hochstadt is emeritus professor of history at Illinois College in Jacksonville, Illinois. He speaks for many in the professoriate today when he boasts, "I have not said that pledge [the Pledge of Allegiance] for many years," owing, he says, to false statements about "liberty and justice for all" found in it. He is particularly angry about the phrase "one nation under God" in the pledge. He brands those words "un-American."[263]

What really gets Hochstadt's goat (and the flocks of his ilk) is the persistence of patriotism in America. An international survey of nineteen countries conducted in 2023 concluded that "the United States is the most patriotic country, with 41% of its respondents answering 'yes' to 'My country is the best country in the world,' and 32% believe that the US is 'better than most countries.'"[264]

The same YouGov poll found that young people, those between the ages of eighteen and twenty-nine, were the least patriotic. So were Democrats.[265] In another 2023 survey,

[263] Steve Hochstadt, "Religion of Patriotism," LA Progressive, September 9, 2020, https://www.laprogressive.com/progressive-issues-religion-of-patriotism/.

[264] "Most Patriotic Countries 2023," World Population Review, https://worldpopulationreview.com/country-rankings-patriotic-countries/.

[265] "YouGov Survey: Americans' Views on Patriotism, June 15–17, 2022—1000 Adult Citizens," YouGov, today.yougov.com.

Gen Z, the youngest adult age group, scored 57 percentage points lower on a patriotic scale than baby boomers.[266]

One obvious reason for this disparity is that many schools have adopted a highly critical perspective of American history in recent years. This is not an accident: it is the result of a determined left-wing agenda promoted by an increasing number of educators. Their intentional efforts are one reason we are so divided as a people. This takes on greater poignancy when we learn from other survey data that it is not the most affluent and highly educated Americans who are the most patriotic — it is the poor, those in the lowest income bracket.[267]

THE AMERICAN CREED RECONSIDERED

Much of the division affecting America today is driven by conflicts over race, and most of it centers on a long history of inequality. To her credit, the Catholic Church's legacy with respect to race is comparatively good — not merely in her teachings but in her deeds. Not only has the Church long condemned slavery — St. Patrick, who was himself enslaved, was the first person in history known to publicly denounce it — but the abolitionist movement could not have succeeded

---

[266] Sonnet Frisbie, "For Gen Z, the Future of Corporate Activism Is Local First, Global Second," Morning Consult, January 9, 2023, https://morningconsult.com/2023/01/9/gen-z-corporate-activism-is-local-first/.

[267] Bill Donohue, *The War on Virtue: How the Ruling Class Is Killing the American Dream* (Manchester, NH: Sophia Institute Press, 2023), 58.

without the reasoning reflected in natural law and in theories of natural rights.

As the *Catechism of the Catholic Church* explains, "Respect for the human person entails respects for the rights that flow from his dignity as a creature. These rights are prior to society and must be recognized by it."[268] Similarly, in 1963 Pope John XXIII wrote in his encyclical *Pacem in Terris* that "all men are equal by reason of their natural dignity," and because of this, "racial discrimination can in no way be justified."[269]

From the period of slavery through to the period of racial inequities of the Jim Crow era, the handicaps placed on African Americans were many and lasting. But beginning in the 1940s, there has been a steady march toward justice and equality, though many in elite quarters seem blind to it.

War is one of the most important, if not the most important, catalysts for social change. The armed forces were integrated shortly after World War II, and it was in 1947 that Major League Baseball accepted Jackie Robinson as the first black man to play the game. In the decade that followed, the historic 1954 decision in *Brown v. Board of Education* ensured that the schools were integrated. In 1955, Rosa Parks became a national figure when she refused to give up her seat to a white passenger, as ordered to do by a white bus driver. It was then that a twenty-six-year-old Baptist preacher, Rev. Martin Luther King Jr., began his civil rights crusade.

---

[268] J. C. A. Garcia, "Racism, Catholic Social Teaching," in *Encyclopedia of Catholic Social Thought*, 291. The references in the *Catechism* are at nos. 1928–1930.
[269] Ibid.

The first meeting held by King to announce a bus boycott drew a crowd of around five thousand. When he spoke, he said he felt that God spoke for him. He took the moral high ground, offering a stirring speech: "If we are wrong, the Supreme Court of this nation is wrong. If we are wrong, the Constitution of the United States is wrong. If we are wrong, God Almighty is wrong.... If we are wrong, justice is a lie.... And we are determined ... to work and fight until justice runs down like water and righteousness like a mighty stream."[270]

After 381 days, the boycott ended in success. But the civil rights movement was just beginning.

The 1957 Civil Rights Act was the first piece of federal civil rights protection since the end of Reconstruction in 1875. In that same year, the city of Little Rock, Arkansas, was mandated by the courts to desegregate the schools. But it was in the next decade that substantive progress was made on a national scale.

On February 1, 1960, four black college students entered a Woolworth store and sat down at a "white" lunch counter. When they were ordered to leave, they conducted a sit-in, a tactic that was later put to widespread use throughout the South. In 1962, James Meredith had to be escorted by thousands of troops when he sought to enter the University of Mississippi. Alabama Governor George Wallace tried, unsuccessfully, to stop a black man and a black woman from entering the University of Alabama;

[270] Myron Magnet, "Like Some Old Prophet of Old," review of *King: A Life*, by Jonathan Eig, *Claremont Review of Books* 23, no. 2 (Spring 2023): 19.

President John F. Kennedy dispatched federal troops to do the job. In 1963, Martin Luther King was imprisoned in a Birmingham jail; it was there that he wrote his magnificent discourse on civil disobedience. In August of 1963, he led the March on Washington, one hundred years after the Emancipation Proclamation. The "I Have a Dream" speech he delivered there assured him a permanent place in American history.

King envisioned a society where black and white children would be able to join hands, and where everyone would be judged by the content of their character, not the color of their skin. After his speech he went to the White House where he was greeted by President John F. Kennedy. The subsequent landmark Civil Rights Act of 1964, and the 1965 Voting Rights Act, were modeled on King's vision.

King was keenly aware that the dream of freedom and equality for all had not been realized. But he also knew that it would come to fruition one day. His optimism was not some Pollyannaish wish. It was rooted in the pledge that the Founders made: all men are created equal. It was up to us to make good on it. What gave King hope is what Samuel Huntington calls the American Creed.

The American Creed, Huntington writes, is not based on an idea; rather, it is based on a belief, the belief in freedom. But freedom does not exist in isolation. When joined with equality, individualism, democracy, and the rule of law under a constitution, we have what he calls the values of the American Creed.

The American Creed is inspiring, but it comes with a price: to ensure that every American accomplishes it is a daunting goal. To put it differently, it has an underside: the gap between the ideals of the American Creed and the reality on the ground can be more than dismaying—it can fuel anger and resentment, especially among intellectuals.

If there was one intellectual in the twentieth century who offered a mature understanding of the inconsistency between the American Creed and the reality of racism and discrimination, it was the Swedish economist Gunnar Myrdal. In 1944, ten years before the ruling in *Brown v. Board of Education*, Myrdal wrote his book *An American Dilemma* (the decision in *Brown* was partially based on his book). He argued that the American Creed was so strong that the disjunction between what it promised and the reality of racial inequality would eventually result in its successful resolution: Myrdal was confident that the stain of racial inequality would be ameliorated. Yes, he said, white racism existed; but America was not racist at its core.

What Myrdal said was undeniably true. But that is not what leftist intellectuals believe. They believe America is irredeemably racist. Furthermore, they blame capitalism for generating inequalities. In essence, they teach students that America is flawed because it has not made good on the American Creed. This perspective is historically myopic. Indeed, it represents a profoundly immature understanding of America.

For many years I taught a class, "Social Problems," that covered a wide range of subjects. The textbooks were invariably shallow, focusing on the conflict between the American Creed and the reality of existing shortcomings. It made no difference what the issue was—race, sex, class—the emphasis was always on structures of inequality and alleged oppression. This interpretation of social problems, I told my students, was like seeing the world as drawn on a blackboard. It was always so neat. The real world, however, is much more complex.

The approach I took was quite different. I compared whatever the social problem was that we were studying to conditions that existed two hundred years ago, one hundred years ago, fifty years ago, and today. Have we made progress in our treatment of blacks, women, the poor—or have we gone backwards? Then I compared current conditions in the United States to current conditions in Latin America, Africa, the Middle East, Asia, and Europe. How do conditions in those parts of the world stack up against conditions here at home?

When social problems were put in historical and cross-cultural perspective, students came away with a much more balanced understanding of American society. My goal was not to show that America is perfect—major shortcomings were dealt with forthrightly. My approach was simply to be honest.

Unfortunately, many left-wing sociologists prefer to compare existing conditions only to fanciful blackboard ideals. They choose that route largely because they are ideologues. There seems to be a personal dimension to their politics: they enjoy basking in negativity; it has the effect of making them feel morally superior. In the end, however, it is dishonest. How so? When studying race relations, or any other social problem, the operative question should always be "Compared to what?"

Zinn's Sordid View of America

One of the most famous left-wing intellectuals in the past half century to take a hypercritical view of America was Howard Zinn. His 1980 book, *A People's History of the United States: 1492–Present*, has sold millions of copies — thanks to professors and school districts that made it assigned reading. It has done more to poison the minds of students than any other single volume. It is the Bible of America-bashers everywhere. And it is deeply flawed. Thanks to Mary Grabar, who wrote *Debunking Howard Zinn: Exposing the Fake History That Turned a Generation against America*, we are able to put his work under a critical microscope.

Not surprisingly, Zinn was an atheist and a Communist. In 1948, an FBI informant reported that Zinn had told him that he was a member of the Communist Party, and that he attended meetings five nights a week. In 1951, Zinn taught Marxism at the Communist Party headquarters in Brooklyn. In 1953, when the FBI confronted him with evidence that he was a member of the Communist Party, he tried to make light of it. But according to Ronald Radosh, who was a Communist for a short period of time in college, and who later exposed many Communists in the United States, Zinn was definitely one of them.[271]

[271] Mary Grabar, *Debunking Howard Zinn* (Washington, D.C.: Regnery, 2019), 42.

In the classroom, Zinn was known for his "spell-binding manner" and for never giving exams; he never failed a student. Graber notes that he "used his teaching podium to agitate, assigning readings and activities that kept students at a high emotional pitch."[272] He was particularly influential during the ruckus days of the 1960s and 1970s. What he taught was more propaganda than empirically verifiable scholarship.

For example, when discussing slavery, Zinn admitted that it existed in Africa, but he hastened to add that the African version was, as Grabar describes it, of a "kinder, gentler kind of slavery." She faults him for "romanticizing life in pre-colonial Africa," thus setting the stage for his biased analysis of the European encounter with Africans.[273]

Zinn's analysis of the Civil War concluded that it was a missed opportunity—the war should have extended to a war on the capitalism that, he contended, undergirded slavery. Without offering any evidence—there isn't any—he made the remarkable argument that racism was an invention of Western culture. Predictably, he took to smearing Lincoln. His students learned that Lincoln was just an opportunist looking for political advantages, not a sincere opponent of slavery. Indeed, he maintained that Lincoln "could not see blacks as equals," despite clear evidence to the contrary.[274]

In the early twentieth century, the National Association for the Advancement of Colored People (NAACP) was

[272] Ibid., 53–54.
[273] Ibid., 90–91.
[274] Ibid., 109.

founded to promote racial equality. It may strike some as surprising to learn that Zinn was not a big fan of the organization. That's because it was too mainstream; it was not sufficiently radical, the way the Communist Party was. He constantly criticized its activities, even though it had achieved remarkable progress in many aspects of American life. The Communist Party went further than Zinn, and in 1931 it actually tried to shut down NAACP meetings.[275]

Zinn was known for projecting his own hatred of America onto blacks. He steadfastly refused to see average black men as patriotic Americans, though clearly they were. During World War II, he insisted that blacks fought in the war simply for a "victory over racism," and not to protect American interests. Even if there is some truth to what he said, the facts show that blacks were far less likely to register as conscientious objectors than whites were.[276]

Similarly, Zinn found it hard to praise President Truman for abetting the cause of racial justice, and claimed that his decisions were not radical enough.[277] He treated Rev. Martin Luther King Jr. the same way. King's historic March on Washington in 1963 was nothing but a "friendly assemblage."[278] As Grabar aptly put it, "If it isn't marked by violence and explosive anger, Zinn can't get excited about it." In the same year Zinn told students that voting doesn't matter, another manifestation of his disdain for reformist

[275] Ibid., 179–186.
[276] Ibid., 132–133.
[277] Ibid., 188.
[278] Ibid., 192.

policies. Again, Grabar sees through this, noting, "It's almost as if Zinn wanted to sabotage the Civil Rights Movement. In fact, the Marxist class struggle, not civil rights for blacks, was his real agenda."[279]

Given the enormous size of his audience, the damage done by Zinn is incalculable. Obedient students, propagandized by their America-hating professors, have been guzzling his moonshine for decades. Zinn's many fans in the professoriate are no less guilty of fanning the flames of anti-Americanism. Even when they attach themselves to new ideological strains, such as multiculturalism, they continue to draw on his work.

MULTICULTURALISM

In its most innocent iteration, multiculturalism represents an attempt to appreciate the multiplicity of racial and ethnic groups throughout American society, and indeed throughout the world. But there is rarely anything innocent about it: it is invariably used as an ideological whip to denigrate Western civilization and to elevate societies that are in every meaningful way inferior to it. At its core, it is designed to divide us as a nation.

Pope Benedict XVI was a steady critic of multiculturalism. He observed that it was "a peculiar Western self-hatred that is nothing short of pathological."[280] The distinguished

[279] Ibid., 194–195.
[280] Joseph Ratzinger and Marcello Pera, *Without Roots: The West, Relativism, Christianity, Islam* (New York: Basic Books, 2008), 78–79. The words quoted are those of Ratzinger.

historian Arthur M. Schlesinger Jr. was more specific: "There is surely no reason for Western civilization to have guilt trips laid on it by champions of cultures based on despotism, superstition, tribalism, and fanaticism."[281] Both men spoke the truth; both men were roundly condemned.

At its base, multiculturalism is a formal rejection of the vision of American society as described by J. Hector St. John de Crèvecoeur in his eighteenth-century classic, *Letters from an American Farmer*. This French student of America had never seen such assimilation: the ability to "melt" disparate peoples into a new man was remarkable and unparalleled. Thus was the idea of America as a "melting pot" born.

People like Horace Mann picked up on this idea in the early nineteenth century. Although the "melting pot" worked quite well on its own, he decided to help stir the pot by arguing to use the public schools to help assimilate different religious and ethnic groups.

From the perspective of multiculturalism, the "melting pot" idea is anathema. That's because the proponents of multiculturalism want to divide us, not unite us.

It is bizarre, to say the least, that the civilization responsible for the greatest achievements in education, art, architecture, science, and economic prosperity is being attacked by the very elites who run it. It is also ironic that they focus so much ire on the one institution that for millennia

---

[281] Arthur M. Schlesinger Jr., *The Disuniting of America: Reflections on a Multicultural Society* (Knoxville, TN: Whittle Direct Books, 1991), 76.

has been the bedrock of Western civilization, namely, the Catholic Church.

Without the Church's triumph over paganism, says sociologist Robert Nisbet, history would look very different. He cogently notes that "had the Christians been defeated by indigenous Greco-Roman gods, by gods imported from the East, or by both, the West would have known only a fraction of the social, economic, cultural and intellectual history that has been a continuous flow from the earliest centuries of Christianity."[282]

Instead of cherishing Christianity, and all that it has contributed to Western civilization, academic elites throw intellectual spitballs at it. That this is happening at the same time that Islam is being revered only shows how intellectually corrupt the proponents of multiculturalism have become.

In 2021, Georgetown University announced to great fanfare that the Jesuits had pledged $100 million to a foundation for the descendants of the 272 enslaved people sold by Maryland Jesuits in 1838. The Jesuit Conference of Canada and the U.S. pledged the money as a down payment on the $1 billion it hopes to raise. Meanwhile, few seem to have noticed that Georgetown today employs a professor who defends slavery and rape—provided the slave masters and rapists are Muslims.

Jonathan Brown is a convert to Islam and holds an endowed chair at Georgetown. The Jesuit-run institution has a

---

[282] Robert Nisbet, *Prejudices* (Cambridge: Harvard University Press, 1982), 47.

wealthy benefactor in Saudi Arabia, a nation that happens to ban Christianity. Incredibly, Brown argues that "slavery cannot just be treated as a moral evil in and of itself." And he really means it. "I don't think it's morally evil to own somebody because we own lots of people all around us." He also believes that for Muslims, what he calls "non-consensual sex" (also known as rape) is okay. He takes umbrage at the Western notion of "consent," maintaining that "it's very hard to have this discussion because we think of, let's say in the modern United States, the *sine qua non* of morally correct sex is consent."[283]

So while Georgetown is receiving plaudits for standing up against long-dead slave-owning Jesuits, it continues to employ a very much alive and noted professor who justifies slavery and rape today. If a Catholic priest did the same thing, it would be front-page news.

Richard Dawkins is a prominent English left-wing biologist and atheist who was disinvited in 2017 by a Berkeley left-wing radio station after it was discovered that he said Islam is the world's "most evil" religion.[284] It did not matter to KPFA that Dawkins has made a career out of bashing Christianity, especially Catholicism. That was laudatory. But it mattered greatly when he condemned Islam.

[283] Jonathan Brown, "Slavery and Islam—Part I: The Problem of Slavery," Yaqeen Institute, February 7, 2017, https://yaqeen-institute.org/timeline/the-problem-of-slavery/.

[284] Bill Donohue, "Why the Left Defends Islamists," Catholic League, August 8, 2017, https://www.catholicleague.org/why-the-left-defends-islamists/.

Why did that bother the Left so much? On the surface, it makes no sense for the Left to embrace Islamists. After all, the Left dreams of a sexual free-for-all, and radical Islamists want burkas on women and nooses on gays. How can libertinism and sharia be squared? Scratch beneath the surface and it quickly becomes apparent that what unites the Left and Islamists is hate: hatred of the West. They hate America, they hate Europe—and they would like to destroy Israel.

It is that animus that compels them to target the Judeo-Christian culture upon which the West was built. That is why they want to gut it. The Left will support *any* movement that seeks to damage the West.

ROMANTICIZING INDIGENOUS PEOPLES

If ever there were proof of the animus against Western civilization that multiculturalists promote, it can be found by studying what the National Education Association (NEA) has said about Columbus.

The NEA is the largest labor union in the nation. It represents more than three million teachers and administrators. It is also a decidedly left-wing organization, and as such often expresses a hypercritical perspective of the United States and Western civilization. Its frontal assault on Columbus is one such example.

On the NEA's website, information about Columbus is found in a section titled "Resources for Teaching about Indigenous Peoples." There is plenty of information about the people who migrated to America—just like the rest of us.

These "indigenous peoples" came from Asia. We know them as American Indians.

The NEA has lots of resources for teachers on Columbus and the Indians, the most prominent of which is the Zinn Education Project. That's right—it's named after Howard Zinn. The goal of this initiative is crystal clear: "Abolishing Columbus Day." The ever-reliable Mary Grabar has something to say about this subject.

One way Zinn created his false history of Columbus was to selectively quote him. Zinn's account is littered with ellipses, glaring omissions that badly distort the words actually written by Columbus.

Just as bad, Zinn lifted much of what he said about Columbus from a book written by his radical friend, Hans Koning. But Koning was not a scholar or a historian—and his slim volume provides no sources, no citations at all, which makes his slanted viewpoint impossible to verify.

Zinn would have the reader believe that the Indians were doing just fine before the Europeans came along. Never once does he attempt to explain why so many tribes engaged in so much savage warfare against each other (the conflict between the Hurons and Iroquois was particularly brutal, but there are many other examples). Nor does he discuss cannibalism, human sacrifice, and the other acts of cruelty that were widespread before the white men arrived.

Just as important, Zinn does not comment on all of the Indians that helped the Europeans by defecting to their side. They had had enough of the butchery they experienced at the hands of their fellow indigenous tribes. None of this is taught to students.[285]

The NEA account does not include the viewpoint of scholars who disagree with Zinn. For example, Carol Delaney, a Stanford University anthropologist, maintains that Columbus acted on his Christian faith and told his crew to be kind to the Indians. Here's a quote from Columbus that students never learn about: "I want the natives to develop a friendly attitude toward us because I know that they are a people who can be made free and converted to our Holy Faith more by love than by force."[286]

America-haters love to bash Thanksgiving. Why? Because radical secularists hate a holiday that has Christian roots.

Not a November goes by without some sage citing the work of Robert Jensen, a retired professor from the University of Texas at Austin. He suggests we scratch Thanksgiving altogether and atone for our sins—by which he means, of course, the alleged sins committed by people who have been dead and buried for centuries.

Here's what Jensen proposes. "One indication of moral progress in the United States would be the replacement of Thanksgiving Day and its self-indulgent family feasting with a National Day of Atonement accompanied by a self-reflective collective fasting." We need to do that, he says, because

[285] Bill Donohue, "NEA's Left-Wing Attack on Columbus," Catholic League, October 6, 2022, https://www.catholicleague.org/neas-left-wing-attack-on-columbus/.

[286] Bill Donohue, "Origins of the Assault on Columbus," Catholic League, October 6, 2021, https://www.catholicleague.org/origins-of-the-assault-on-columbus/.

of the "massacre of hundreds of Pequot Indian men, women and children" at the hands of the English.[287]

Historian Thomas E. Woods Jr. dispelled Jensen's myth in his bestselling book *The Politically Incorrect Guide to American History.*

The Pequots were never a large tribe, and they were never wiped out by the Puritans. Their descendants are recognized today by the federal government and are one of the recognized tribes in Connecticut. The Puritans had political rights to Indian lands, but never property rights. In fact, as Woods makes clear, "The colonial governments actually punished individuals who made unauthorized acquisitions of Indian lands."[288]

Moreover, each colony worked cooperatively with the Indians to secure land, offering metal knives and hoes as well as clothing and jewelry. "The Puritans recognized Indian hunting and fishing rights *on lands that the Indians had sold to them*," writes Woods.[289]

Then there are the Catholic roots to Thanksgiving that Jensen and his peers do not want to discuss. Eric Metaxas has done the best work on this subject, recalling the travails and triumphs of Squanto, a brave Patuxent Indian boy.

In 1608, when Squanto was twelve years old, he was kidnapped by English colonists and was taken to Spain as a slave. Fortunately for him, some monks bought him—then they

[287] Bill Donohue, "The Assault on Thanksgiving," Catholic League, November 23, 2021, https://www.catholicleague.org/the-assault-on-thanksgiving/.
[288] Ibid.
[289] Ibid.

cared for him, taught him their language, and introduced him to Christianity. The monks knew that the young Indian, now Catholic, wanted to go back to America; so they sent him to live with a London merchant, John Slanie, and his family. He learned English well, and after spending five years with the family, he boarded a ship to America.

Squanto arrived in Plymouth, Massachusetts, which is where he grew up. He was stunned by what he found: everyone he knew was dead.

Contrary to what left-wing authors say, they were not bludgeoned to death. They died of smallpox. According to Metaxas, the Pilgrims "basically adopted him." Lucky for them, he spoke English and was able to help them.

Indeed, Squanto "showed them everything there was to know. He showed them how to catch fish, where the lobsters were, how to tread the eels out of the mud in the stream beds. He basically single-handedly showed them how to survive." Governor William Bradford of the Plymouth colony wrote in his journal that Squanto was a special person sent by God.[290]

As a tribute to the bond they had established, Squanto and the Pilgrims celebrated a Thanksgiving dinner. The custom originated in 1621 when Bradford recognized a day of public praise and prayer after the first harvest. The first national observance did not occur until President Washington, at the request of Congress, named Thursday, November 26, 1789, as a "day of public thanksgiving and prayer."

[290] Ibid.

The Left does not want us to acknowledge the truth about Thanksgiving. That would undercut their America-bashing agenda. They also don't want us to know why so many American Indians died.

Noted historian William D. Rubinstein, in his masterful book *Genocide*, writes that

> recent historians sympathetic to the plight of the American Indians at the hand of European settlers from 1492 onwards have repeatedly noted that while 95 percent of Indians living in the America perished (according to those historians) over the century or so after the coming of the white man, most of this diminution in population occurred through such factors as the importation of virulent diseases previously unknown in the Americas, the destruction of settled life-styles, enslavement, and the psychological effects of conquest rather than through overt murders and slaughters, although plenty of these took place.[291]

We are also being lied to by activist professors who portray all the Europeans as oppressors and all indigenous people as gentle and earth-loving. The historical fact is that there were kind Europeans and cruel Europeans. There were also kind Indians and cruel Indians. To focus almost exclusively

[291] Bill Donohue, "The Dark Side of Indigenous Peoples," Catholic League, October 8, 2021, https://www.catholicleague.org/the-dark-side-of-indigenous-peoples/.

on the worst aspects of the Europeans, and the best traits of the indigenous people, is a political exercise; it is not a historical reality. History is complicated, though not in the mind of left-wing ideologues. The fact is, a lot of blood has been spilt by virtually every people that has ever walked the face of the earth. And too often, yesterday's oppressed became tomorrow's oppressors. That is the dirty, dark truth of history.

Douglas Murray is a wise social observer who is onto the game of romanticizing indigenous peoples. He notes that "non-Western countries are able to get away with contemporary crimes as monstrous as anything that has happened in the Western past."[292] This is what happens when objective analysis gives way to subjective interpretations of history. It is at the heart of the multicultural fallacy.

TRASHING THE PAST

As a veteran, I was sickened by the recent sight of young people tearing down monuments of historical figures, all in the name of social justice. That they were sometimes egged on by government officials made matters even worse.

The current preoccupation with tarring figures in American history is an example of selectively applying today's standards to past behaviors. This is historically unfair; it is being done to foster a particular political agenda. Its goal is to condemn certain demographic groups — white male heterosexual Christians, in particular — while

[292] Douglas Murray, *The War on the West* (New York: Broadside Books, 2022), 9.

providing a mantle of moral superiority to those groups now on the rise. It is also being done to promote the grievance industry, which serves the "divide and conquer" campaign.

I testified before the New York City Mayoral Advisory Commission on Art, Monuments, and Markers on Thanksgiving Eve, November 22, 2017. Most of those who testified before the panel were there to argue that monuments on public grounds of controversial public figures, such as Columbus, should be taken down; and the audience was overwhelmingly on their side. I chose a different route. I sought to convince them that some of the historical figures we herald today as moral beacons were actually virulently anti-Catholic bigots. This raised the obvious question: Do we tear down their statues as well?

The figure I chose was Frederick Douglass, one of the most revered persons in American history today. There are many reasons to applaud what he did. But as with so many other public figures, there was another side to him.

Douglass was an ex-slave, an abolitionist, and a supporter of women's rights. Unbeknownst to most, he was also an anti-Catholic bigot. In his weekly publication, the *Douglass Papers*, he often spoke of "the prevalence and power to the Christian Church and religion at Rome and of the strange things they believed and practiced there in the way of religious rites and ceremonies."[293]

---

[293] Bill Donohue, "War on Monuments Is Driven by Hate," Catholic League, November 28, 2017, https://www.catholicleague. org/war-on-monuments-is-driven-by-hate/.

Douglass held a particular animus against Irish Catholics, blaming them, not the English, for their own plight: it was the religious bigotry of Irish Catholics that was responsible for their own condition. He was in Ireland in 1845 when the English stole food from the Irish during the famine, yet he never objected. The Irish may have had some things in common with blacks, he said, but in the end they were pawns of "Romanism," that nefarious force that brought "ignorance, cunning, and crimes" to Ireland.[294]

After making my case against Douglass, I emphasized that I did not want the statue of him removed from Central Park. I explicitly condemned all attempts at cultural cleansing. The room was silent.

I tried to make two points. First, removing monuments and statues of historical figures is a very dangerous road to go down. Is there any public figure — or for that matter any private person — who is so squeaky-clean that he has nothing to regret? Not only that, but those leading the charge against time-honored Americans, such as the mayor of New York City at that time, Bill de Blasio, routinely prove just how thoroughly imperfect they themselves are.

In making my second point, I said a mature understanding of Douglass would commend him for his contributions, while recognizing his anti-Catholic bigotry (a trait he shared with many other abolitionists). He had done great good, I said, and the times in which he lived were different, so to indict him on the basis of his anti-Catholic sentiments (he

[294] Ibid.

said the Church was "Satan"), without noting his abolitionist efforts, would be simply unfair.[295]

Judging the past by the standards of today is morally seductive. But it smacks of hubris. Future generations may well look back at what we are doing today—to the unborn and to the sexually confused—and render harsh judgments against us.

FROM KING TO KENDI

The 1964 Civil Rights Act was the most important and comprehensive civil rights legislation in the twentieth century. Discrimination on the basis of race, color, religion, and national origin was banned. The goal was to provide equal opportunity for every American, and section 703(j) of Title VII explicitly barred preferential treatment. But it didn't take long for the courts and administrative agencies to start ignoring this provision. The big turning point came when President Lyndon Johnson gave the 1965 commencement address at Howard University.

A Southerner, Johnson was acutely aware of our nation's historic discrimination against African Americans, and he wanted to set it right. In his address, he rejected the core principle of equal opportunity that undergirded the Civil Rights Act, passed only a year earlier. Instead, he called for equality of results.

[295] Bill Donohue, "NYC Hearing on Monuments Was Disturbing," Catholic League, November 30, 2017, https://www.catholicleague.org/nyc-hearing-on-monuments-was-disturbing/.

"You do not take a person who, for years, has been hobbled by chains and liberate him, bring him up to the starting line of a race and then say, 'you are free to compete with all the others,' and still justly believe that you have been completely fair," Johnson said. He announced what would be "the next and the more profound stage of the battle for civil rights," and by that he meant "not just equality as a right and a theory but equality as a fact and equality as a result."[296]

Equality of result is a daunting, and dangerous, goal. It has proven to be extraordinarily controversial as well. This was the beginning of affirmative action. Initially, it meant that employers had to affirmatively set out to hire qualified minorities, and to favor racial minorities *if all else were equal*. But all else is never equal; the world is too varied to measure qualifications that precisely. Soon the hopeful goals and aspirational timetables that had been established turned into quotas. Inevitably, that led to discrimination against non-black people. It was not until 2023 that the Supreme Court, ruling on a case brought by Asian Americans, finally struck down affirmative action in a 6–3 decision. The high court said that Harvard and the University of North Carolina had violated the "the guarantees of the Equal Protection Clause" of the Fourteenth Amendment by discriminating against Asian students in their admission process.

[296] Lyndon B. Johnson, "Commencement Address at Howard University: 'To Fulfill These Rights,'" June 4, 1965, Lyndon Baines Johnson Library and Museum, National Archives and Records Administration.

But goals like equal opportunity, even equal results, seem quaint given the current onslaught of critical race theory (CRT). Ostensibly formulated to combat racism, this doctrine insists that all white people are inherently racist—and, as a result, it is inherently racist itself. And it smacks of the radical secular agenda.

The Catholic Church has long rejected radical egalitarianism. In 1884, Pope Leo XIII maintained that while all men had a common origin and nature, they were not equal in terms of their abilities. That is why attempts to mandate "complete equality," he said, were "repugnant to reason."[297]

CRT vehemently rejects the pope's views. CRT holds that the only way to correct past discrimination against blacks is to practice current and future discrimination against whites. In other words, CRT effectively dismisses the rights of the individual, maintaining that even though white people today are in no way responsible for slavery and Jim Crow, they should be discriminated against because they belong to a group that once was. This idea is profoundly at odds with Catholic social ethics, and it is plainly and emphatically un-American.

Moreover, from a Catholic perspective, CRT is hopelessly divisive, and it undercuts the age-old quest for unity and the common good. It must be stressed, too, that the divisiveness is not an unanticipated consequence of CRT. It is central to its ideology. For example, when students in Virginia's West Springfield High School were forced to watch a

[297] Leo XIII, encyclical letter *Humanum Genus* (April 20, 1884), no. 26.

video depicting white people as blood-sucking, cartoon mosquitoes who must be destroyed by non-white people wielding flamethrowers—as happened in 2023—the "divide and conquer" strategy of school officials could not be more evident.[298]

Ibram X. Kendi is one of the most influential proponents of CRT. Where Martin Luther King Jr. took the high road in tackling racism, Kendi takes the low road.

"When I see racial disparities," he says, "I see racism."[299] Perhaps he is thinking that racism is the reason most professional hockey players are white? But then it must also be the reason most professional basketball players are black. In fact, it must explain why most jockeys are Hispanic. But does anyone really believe this to be true, other than CRT zealots? There are plenty of good reasons racial disparities exist, reasons that have nothing to do with race.

Robin DiAngelo is another CRT fanatic. She and Kendi believe they are embarked on a human rights crusade that will fundamentally change not only American society but human nature. This rejection of a core Judeo-Christian tenet—that human nature is bequeathed by God and does not change—makes them splendid

---

[298] Carrie Sheffield, "Critical Race Theory Is Teaching Kids to Hate Each Other," *New York Post*, March 9, 2023, https://nypost.com/2023/03/08/critical-race-theory-is-teaching-kids-to-hate-each-other/.

[299] Christopher F. Rufo, "Ibram X. Kendi Is the False Prophet of a Dangerous and Lucrative Faith," *New York Post*, July 23, 2021, https://nypost.com/2021/07/22/ibram-x-kendi-is-the-false-prophet-of-a-dangerous-and-lucrative-faith/.

examples of what happens when secular ideas are taken to extremes. "We will change the way human nature functions," they write. "We will change human nature."[300] Like so many other utopians in history, they have ambitions that are not only unrealizable but also wreak havoc when attempts are made to achieve them.

The divisive and damaging force of CRT is really apparent when it is applied in real-life circumstances.

When the State University of New York at Albany enacted a library internship program that formally excluded white students, it triggered a complaint by the Equal Protection Project. The internship offered $1,500 scholarships and up to $11,500 in stipends to "black graduates of master library and information science ... or master of science in information systems." The program was launched in 2020, three years before a federal civil rights complaint was made. SUNY Albany defended the program in the name of "diversity."[301]

Texas A&M University set aside $2 million in 2022 to be spent on bonuses to attract "faculty of color." Some were awarded $100,000. Not only were white students told they

[300] Rachel del Guidice, "What's behind 'the Plot to Change America,'" Daily Signal, July 29, 2020, https://dailysignal.com/2020/07/29/whats-behind-the-plot-to-change-america/.

[301] Carl Campanile, "SUNY Albany Faces Federal Race-Discrimination Complaint over Black-Only Internships," *New York Post*, June 11, 2023, https://nypost.com/2023/06/11/suny-albany-faces-federal-race-discrimination-complaint-for-black-only-internships/.

could not apply, but Asians were told they couldn't either.[302]
The University of North Carolina at Chapel Hill, which had
its affirmative action admissions program shut down by the
Supreme Court, instituted a Fellowship for Exploring Research in Nutrition that explicitly excluded white applicants.
Fellows earned thousands of dollars and were housed in on-
campus apartments paid for by the university. They also
received generous mentorship opportunities, including letters of recommendation.[303]

CRT is being taught in the U.S. Air Force Academy, West
Point, the U.S. Naval Academy, the U.S. Merchant Marine
Academy, and the U.S. Coast Guard Academy. The elite
medical schools are on board, too, as is the American College
of Surgeons. This new kind of racism—and that is what it
is—is being tolerated and promoted by people who have allowed their compassion to create a new form of injustice.

THE "NEW APARTHEID"

The increasing balkanization of American society has had the
effect of treating racial and ethnic groups as if they were members of different tribes. Some want it that way. DiAngelo, the
author of the bestselling book *White Fragility*, certainly does.

---

[302] Aaron Sibarium, "Nation's Largest Public University Hit with
Class Action Suit over Race-Based Hiring Practices," Free Beacon, September 13, 2022, https://freebeacon.com/campus/
nations/largest/public-university-hit-with-class-action-suit-over-
race-based-hiring-practices/.

[303] Aaron Sibarium, "White Students Are Prohibited from Applying
to This UNC Fellowship," Free Beacon, December 19, 2022,
https://freebeacon.com/campus-white-students-are-prohibited-
from-applying-to-this-unc-fellowship/.

"People of color need to get away from white people and have some community with each other."[304] No doubt the Klan would agree. And so does Harvard University. That is why it designated "an exclusive space for Black-identifying audience members" when an adaptation of *Macbeth* was performed in 2021.[305]

Welcome to the world of the "new apartheid." The much condemned South African practice of separating the races is now very much accepted in the United States. It is not the average American who likes segregating whites and blacks—it is the ruling class. The elites who run our institutions are the champions of the "new apartheid."

According to a study of 173 public and private colleges and universities conducted by the National Association of Scholars, 43 percent had programs to segregate student housing by race or sexual orientation, and 46 percent of schools had racially segregated orientation programs. Another 76 percent of the schools had segregated graduation ceremonies. Columbia University, for instance, has six separate graduation ceremonies for students based on race, sexuality, and income level.[306]

Militant secularism is driving much of the segregation. Christianity emphasizes the fact that all people are equal before God. But the same people bloviating about "white

[304] Kristine Parks, "'White Fragility' Author Warns People of Color to 'Get Away from White People,'" Fox News, March 20, 2023, https://www.foxnews.com/media/white-fragility-author-warns-people-color-get-away-white-people/.

[305] Christian Schneider, "Colleges Turn to Segregation to Solve Racial Ills," *National Review*, December 1, 2022, http://www.nationalreview.com/2022/12/colleges-turn-to-segregation-to-solve-racial-ills/.

[306] Ibid.

supremacy" are the ones attacking "Christian privilege." The campuses are now dotted with classes, workshops, and lectures on this subject. At George Washington University, diversity workshops teach that "Christians enjoy a privileged, easier life than their non-Christian counterparts, and that Christians possess 'built-in-advantages' today." In other words, the often-Christian Hispanics who clean the toilets of filthy-rich atheist students and their pampered professors are the "privileged" ones.[307]

At Rutgers University, a guest lecturer from Fairleigh Dickinson University, Khyati Joshi, told students that "Christian privilege" was responsible for slavery.[308] She did not say who is responsible for slavery in the non-white world today.

Florida State University has one of the most extensive diversity programs in the nation. Students are required in some classes to list their "identities." One student was instructed to list himself as a white heterosexual Catholic male. To what end? The point of the assignment, everyone knew, was to shame him. Another student, a female, said that her professor was known for going off on "white privilege" and "systemic racism," and that if any students disagreed with him, their grades would suffer. In fact, when she wrote a paper defending Christianity as an institution that helped to end slavery, she received an F.[309]

[307] Bill Donohue, "Christian Bashing on Campus," Catholic League, February 21, 2023, https://www.catholicleague.org/christian-bashing-on-campus/.
[308] Ibid.
[309] Ibid.

The diversity, equity, and inclusion gurus on campus have training programs where participants learn the four expressions of "religious oppression," all of which blame white Christians for oppressing everyone else.[310] This narrative never explores the bloody history of Indian and African and Middle Eastern tribes.

The proponents of this left-wing agenda talk of "Christian privilege," which is "the view that Christian beliefs, language, and practices do not require any special effort to be recognized, as they are embedded into the U.S. American culture."[311] They decry the celebration of Christmas as a mark of Christian hegemony.

Leaving aside the fact that there is no such thing as a "Christian language," why should it be considered controversial for a nation founded by Christians to celebrate its history? Countries founded by Jews, Hindus, and Muslims celebrate their holy days.

Some classroom discussions at Florida State include an appraisal of the "matrix of oppression," or what some call a "matrix of domination." It is basically a list of victimizers (white male heterosexual Christians) and victims (their counterparts).[312] It would be funny if it weren't so damaging to the young minds and the public square.

None of this has anything to do with the most important goal for which higher education is intended—namely, the pursuit of truth. It has everything to do with thought control and

[310] Ibid.
[311] Ibid.
[312] Ibid.

CULTURAL MELTDOWN

with dividing individuals according to group characteristics. Not surprisingly, campus diversity programs have utterly failed at their purported goal of improving relationships between groups.

Two scholars who have studied this issue in depth, Jay P. Greene and James D. Paul, concluded that the diversity bureaucracies on campus are associated with *worse* rather than better intergroup relations.[313] Political scientist Scott Yenor came to the same conclusion after he studied the impact of diversity programs at Texas A&M University. After eight years of promoting the diversity, equity, and inclusion agenda—with programs that tell blacks they will never get a fair shake and tell whites they are irredeemably racist—the percentage of both black and white students who felt they "belonged" at the university dropped considerably. "The reaction reveals that [the Texas A&M] DEI regime has never been about making everyone feel welcome on campus," Yenor said. "It has been about imposing leftist ideology on everyone, so that activists would dominate the campus life. And indeed, people feel less welcome and activists feel more empowered to spread their cancerous ideologies."[314]

Another divisive goal pushed by the Left is reparations. The purpose of reparations is supposedly to make up for past

---

[313] Jay P. Greene and James D. Paul, "Diversity Industry: DEI Bloat in the Academy," Heritage Foundation, July 27, 2021, https://www.heritage.org/education/report/diversity-university-dei-bloat-the-academy/.

[314] "DEI Is Poisoning College Campuses," *Washington Examiner*, February 27, 2023, https://www.washingtonexaminer.com/restoring-america-/equality-not-elitism/dei-is-poisoning-college-campuses/.

inequities that stopped blacks from making economic progress. But it primarily serves the power politics of grievance.

One of the most cited ways blacks were formerly held back was the practice of "redlining." In 1934, the National Housing Act established the Federal Housing Administration (FHA) to facilitate the financing of homes. The new law guaranteed private mortgages, and it worked: between 1934 and 1972, the percentage of American families that were able to buy a new home rose from 44 percent to 63 percent. The FHA did have a provision that required underwriters to consider a neighborhood's "economic stability" and its "protection from adverse influences." This resulted in what was called redlining; banks declared entire communities ineligible for FHA loans.[315]

Proponents of reparations say redlining hurt blacks the most. However, research by economists William J. Collins and Robert A. Mango shows that between 1940 and 1980, homeownership climbed 37 percent for blacks and 34 percent for whites. Another study showed that "the vast majority (92 percent) of the total redlined home-owning population was white." This prompted Jason Riley of the *Wall Street Journal* to ask, "If being a victim of redlining is a qualification for reparations, what is the argument for excluding whites?"[316]

California Governor Gavin Newsom was more enthusiastic about reparations until a reparations task force said it could top $800 billion. In 2023, that amounted to more than 2.5 times

---

[315] Jason Riley, "The Trouble with Reparations for Redlining," *Wall Street Journal*, June 27, 2023, https://www.wsj.com/articles/ the-trouble-with-reparations-for-redlining-the-mortgages- discrimination-housing-race-f767a2b1/.

[316] Ibid.

the state's annual budget. Money has a way of sobering people up quickly. But money aside, there are other considerations, historic and moral, that make reparations a much more complex policy issue than its proponents like to acknowledge. Moreover, a poll by the University of California Berkeley Institute of Governmental Studies found in the fall of 2023 that voters in California oppose reparations by a two-to-one margin.

Hilary Fordwich, an English global consultant, engaged CNN's Don Lemon in an exchange on this subject that proved to be embarrassing for Lemon. He pressed her on the need for England to provide reparations to Africans for the role the English played in the slave trade. "If reparations need to be paid," Fordwich said, "we need to go right back to the beginning of that supply chain and say, who was rounding up their own people and having them handcuffed in cages." Lemon was startled. "That was in Africa," she said. "The first nation in the world to abolish it [slavery], it was started by William Wilberforce, was the British. In Great Britain, they abolished slavery. Two thousand naval men died on the high seas trying to stop slavery. Why? Because the African kings were rounding up their own people. They had them in cages waiting in the beaches. No one was running into Africa to get them."[317]

There is also the question of whether Africa should pay reparations to white people. It is estimated by scholars that

[317] The interview aired on CNN, September 10, 2022. See "CNN Royal Correspondent Tells Don Lemon Reparations SHOULD Be Paid for Slavery—by Africans," https://www.msn.com/en-us/tv/news/watch-cnn-royal-correspondent-tells-don-lemon-reparations-should-be-paid-for-slavery-e2-80-93-by-africans/ar-A/.

between 1530 and 1780, there were between 1 million and 1.25 million white European Christians enslaved by the Muslims of the Barbary Coast. As economist Thomas Sowell notes, that number "exceeded the number of Africans enslaved in the United States and in the American colonies put together." What are we going to do about that? Sowell gets it right when he says, "Nobody is going to North Africa for reparations, because nobody is going to be fool enough to give it to them."[318]

RACISM, REAL AND CONTRIVED

Left-wing secularists are convinced that most white people are racists, and that religious conservatives are the worst of the lot. They are wrong. Here's a thought experiment:

Let's say Jones is a guy who occasionally tells racist bar jokes. Smith, on the other hand, is a better educated guy who never tells racist jokes, and indeed bristles when he hears them. From all appearances, Jones is the racist. But what if Jones is known for going out of his way to help blacks in need, whether they be co-workers or drivers stranded on the side of the road with a flat tire? And what if Smith has no history of volunteering to help blacks in need, believing that is the job of government? Furthermore, what if Jones works in campaigns to promote school choice, and does so because he wants to give blacks the opportunity to escape failing public schools? And what if Smith opposes

---

[318] Bill Donohue, "Do White Christians Deserve Reparations?," Catholic League, July 15, 2021, https://www.catholicleague.org/do-white-christians-deserve-reparations/.

those initiatives, consigning blacks to schools he wouldn't send his own children to?

Who is the real racist, Jones or Smith? Life is not as neat as some — especially those who look down on the average American — would have us believe.

Steph Curry is an NBA superstar and a big fan of President Biden. In 2023, he was given the Kareem Abdul-Jabbar Social Justice Champion Award. But when he learned that low-income multifamily housing units were to be built near his mansion in Atherton, California, he campaigned against it. He had just bought a $30 million, two-acre, 17,800-square-foot house with seven bedrooms, nine baths, a movie theater, a full bar, a wine cellar, a pool, and a sundeck.

Curry and his wife made no bones about their concerns. In a letter they wrote to the city about a hearing on the low-income housing units, they said, "We hesitate to add to the 'not in our backyard' rhetoric, but we wanted to send a note before today's meeting. Safety and privacy for us and our kids continues to be our top priority and one of the biggest reasons we chose Atherton as home."[319]

In fairness, who can blame the Currys for acting like everyone else? No one wants to see their neighborhood go south. But when Mr. Social Justice is the one

[319] Warner Todd Huston, "Biden Supporter and Woke NBA Player Steph Curry Wants to Block Affordable Housing Being Built near His $30M Mansion," Breitbart, January 31, 2023, https://www.brietbart.com/sports/2023/01/31/biden-supporter-and-woke-nba-player-steph-curry-wants-to-block-affordable-housing-being-built-near-his-30m-mansion/.

complaining—literally citing NIMBY ("not in my back-yard") concerns—it's fair to ask what the public reaction would have been if a white conservative had written such a letter. In Steph's case, there was no outrage. There never seems to be outrage when those on the Left indulge in behavior for which they are so quick to condemn others.

When left-wing professors talk about racism and condemn "white America," they are careful not to say anything derogatory about their heroes, such as Karl Marx. Like Curry, who gave himself a pass, they give Marx a pass.

But consider what Paul Kengor wrote in his seminal book, *The Devil and Karl Marx*: "Karl Marx was a racist who cast freely with choice epithets aimed at blacks and even Jews—ironic given that Marx was an ethnic Jew." Jews, Marx said, were known for "haggling," and for making money their "worldly God." Marx concluded that the world would be better off without them. "The emancipation of the Jews, in the final analysis," he wrote, "is the emancipation of mankind from Judaism." Not to be outdone, he referred to his colleague, Ferdinand Lassalle, as a "greasy Jew," "the little kike," and "the Jewish Nigger." He was known for dropping the "N-word" on many occasions.[320]

None of this matters to Marx's followers, so enamored are they of him for his hatred of capitalism. But it should matter to anyone who is truly concerned about racism.

[320] Paul Kengor, *The Devil and Karl Marx: Communism's Long March of Death, Deception, and Infiltration* (Gastonia, NC: TAN Books, 2020), 86–88.

Major League Baseball moved the All-Star Game from Georgia to Colorado in 2021 to protest what its woke commissioner, Rob Manfred, said were racist election laws. But when the midterm elections were held in November 2022, a poll by the University of Georgia could not find even one black person who said he had a poor experience. The poll found that among black voters, 73 percent said they had an "excellent" experience; the same number was true for white voters. The governor, Brian Kemp, said it best: "Yet again, the myth of voter suppression in Georgia fails to be supported by a shred of evidence."[321]

Our obsession with race makes it difficult for us to see bigotry of a nonracial kind. For example, consider what happened to Dolores Grier, who was an official at the Archdiocese of New York under Cardinal John O'Connor.

Dolores was a devout black Catholic woman. When I first met her in 1994, she explained why she wanted to join the advisory board of the Catholic League. When she was around seventeen, she went for a job interview. After leaving the room somewhat despondent, she told the secretary that she had not gotten the job. The secretary knew exactly why, and told her, "They didn't want you." She asked, "Because I'm black?" No, she said, "because you're Catholic."

Those who are obsessed with race—they are usually white people—cannot understand why more blacks don't

---

[321] Ashley Oliver, "Poll: 0% of Black Voters Say They Had a Poor Experience Voting in Georgia," Breitbart, January 23, 2023, https://www.breitbart.com/politics/2023/01/23/poll-0-black-voters-say-they-had-poor-experience-voting-georgia/.

seem to be as obsessed with race. In 2022, when the Tampa Bay Buccaneers were scheduled to play the Pittsburgh Steelers, a white reporter for ESPN was struck by the fact that the two football coaches—Todd Bowles for the Bucs and Mike Tomlin for the Steelers—were black.

The reporter, Jenna Laine, said to Bowles, "You and Mike Tomlin are the few black head coaches in the league. I wonder what your relationship is like with him and your thoughts about Steve Wilkes joining that?" (Wilkes had recently been named the interim coach for the Carolina Panthers.) Bowles said he had a very good relationship with Tomlin, adding that "we don't look at what color we are" when the game begins. "I have a lot of very good white friends that coach in this league as well," Bowles said, "and I don't think it's a big deal."[322]

Laine wouldn't give up. She asked Bowles if he understood that "representation matters" in the NFL. "You have aspiring coaches and football players, they see you guys—they see someone that looks like them, maybe grew up like them," she said. "That has to mean something." Bowles had had it with her racial obsession. "When you say, 'you guys,' and 'look like them,' and 'grew up like them,' it means that we're oddballs to begin with. And I think the minute you guys stop making a big deal about it, everybody else will as well."

[322] Brian Flood, "Conservatives Celebrate Bucs Coach Todd Bowles Comments Smacking Down ESPN Reporter's Race Question," Fox News, October 14, 2022, https://www.foxnews.com/media/conservatives-celebrate-bucs-coach-todd-bowles-comments-smacking-down-espn-reporters-race-question/.

This obsession is itself a reflection of the mindset of those who are bent on dividing Americans. Benedict Beckeld put his finger on the problem when he noted that it is the progress that we have made in the West that is the heart of the issue. The title of his book, *Western Self-Contempt*, says it all. "Paradoxically ... the lack of confidence in one's own culture arises precisely from that culture's success. The more overwhelming progress is, the greater the perceived gulf will be between the vanguard of that progress and those who feel left out."[323] He puts the blame where it belongs, on the dons of higher education. They typically live a privileged lifestyle, lack common sense, evince less loyalty to their culture's traditions, and are completely self-absorbed.

Yes, to a large degree it is our success that gnaws at hypercritical elites. Andrew Sullivan, the British transplant scholar, stunned Jon Stewart when he opined about America's greatness. "America in 2022 is the most multiracial, multicultural, tolerant, diverse melting pot that has ever existed on planet earth, and there is no place on earth even like it. That's why 86 percent of our immigrants are non-white. Do you think they want to come to a white supremacist country?" Stewart's only reply was to trot out the issue of slavery, as if that refuted Sullivan.[324]

---

[323] William L. Howard, "Does the West Hate Itself?," *Academic Questions* 35, no. 4 (2022): 125. This quarterly journal is published by the National Association of Scholars.

[324] Bill Donohue, "Jon Stewart's Phony Tirade about Racism," Catholic League, March 31, 2022, https://www.catholicleague.org/jon-stewarts-phony-tirade-about-racism/.

The despondency that marks elitist critics of America is a function of their belief in human perfectibility and their refusal to accept the reality that human beings are inherently flawed. Instead of acknowledging that, despite our flaws, we have made great progress in achieving racial equality, and recognizing how much better off minorities are in the United States compared to nations around the world, the ruling class wallows in negativity. It is their secularism that drives elite critics to put their hopes in utopian schemes. As we will see in the next chapter, the pursuit of perfection is a recipe for disaster.

CHAPTER 6

THE ROOT CAUSE OF OUR DISCONTENT

THE ALLURE OF SOCIALISM

THE ROOT CAUSE OF the discontent experienced by left-wing intellectuals lies in their seriously flawed understanding of human nature. The secular vision, which rejects nature and nature's God, allows for a total misunderstanding of the individual and society. To be exact, the secular worldview holds that man is basically good, and our social ills are not so much a reflection of who we are but of the kind of society we have created. This view could not be more radically different than the Christian vision that, owing to our nature, human perfectibility is not possible. For Christians, Heaven awaits the faithful; for secularists, Heaven can be achieved on earth.

Secularists put their faith in the state. In fact, secularists believe that the state has the power to transform human nature, and ultimately society. It is this utopian impulse that has driven so many intellectuals into the socialist camp.

"It is a historical fact that large numbers of prominent (and less prominent) Western intellectuals have been (or were) sympathetic, with varying degrees of intensity and duration, toward regimes they perceived as socialist and intent on implementing the most idealistic teachings of Marxism."[325] Those are the words of sociologist Paul Hollander, one of the most astute scholars who has studied intellectuals.

I witnessed the attraction that Marxism had on my fellow students when I was studying for my Ph.D. in sociology at New York University. I recall many instances when students sat on the floor, legs crossed, listening in awe to a guest lecturer speaking about Marx. They were positively mesmerized by what he said. These totally secular students had finally found their religion: Marxism. As they became more and more faithful, they reacted with hostility to anyone who pointed out the inherent flaws in Marx's writings. When it was shown that Marx's most famous prophecies were proven to be historically wrong, they insisted that his critics were wrong. "That's not what Marx meant" was the most common refrain offered by his apologists. In short, Marx was never wrong. He was their god.

The Catholic tradition, of course, eschews the materialism of Marxism. It is also critical of socialism, though it is cautious about making a full-throated defense of capitalism.

Writing eight years after Marx's death in 1883, Pope Leo XIII in *Rerum Novarum* foresaw the horrors that Marx's ideology would deliver. The socialist utopia was an ill-conceived idea, promoted by those who put their faith in a secular

[325] Paul Hollander, *Political Pilgrims: Travels of Western Intellectuals to the Soviet Union, China, and Cuba 1928–1978* (New York: Oxford University Press, 1981), 26.

ideology. The pope did not mince words and said that "ideal equality about which they entertain pleasant dreams would be in reality the leveling down of all to a like condition of misery and degradation."[326] What he described came through in the twentieth century. The victims of Marxism are legion.

In that same encyclical, Leo made the case for private property. In doing so, he did not take a laissez-faire position. Leo, along with Pius XI in *Quadragesimo Anno* (1931), was concerned about the individualistic premises of capitalism, and both popes called for reforms.[327] Their idea of the good society rests on a market economy, but one tempered by Christian principles. Still, if capitalism had to be reformed, socialism was fundamentally flawed and incapable of reformation.

Pius XII was adamant in his insistence that socialism would give the state the kind of power that would destroy freedom. "A sound democracy, based on the immutable principles of the natural law and revealed truth," he said, "will resolutely turn its back on such corruption as gives to the state an unchecked and unlimited power, and moreover makes of the democratic regime, notwithstanding an outward show to the contrary, purely and simply a form of

---

[326] Peter A. Kwasniewski, "Equality/Inequality," in *Encyclopedia of Catholic Social Thought, Social Science, and Social Policy*, ed. Michael L. Coulter, Stephen M. Krason, Richard S. Myers, and Joseph Varacalli (Lanham, MD: Scarecrow Press, 2007), 366.

[327] Francis Canavan, S.J., "The Image of Man in Catholic Thought," in *Catholicism, Liberalism, and Communitarianism: The Catholic Intellectual Tradition and the Moral Foundations of Democracy*, ed. Kenneth L. Grasso, Gerard V. Bradley, and Robert P. Hunt (Lanham, MD: Rowman & Littlefield, 1995), 16.

absolutism."[328] What happened in the Soviet Union, and what was beginning to take shape in Communist China, proved his prescience.

Why socialism was destined to fail was best understood by St. John Paul II. It was not a matter of poor policy choices. Rather, it was built into the very DNA of socialism. "The fundamental error of socialism is anthropological in nature. Socialism considers the individual person simply as an element, a molecule within the social organism, so that the good of the individual is completely subordinated to the functioning of the socio-economic mechanism."[329]

As his predecessors did, John Paul II understood that free market capitalism was not a panacea, but had to be tailored to achieve the common good. He stressed that "the free market is the most effective instrument for utilizing resources and responding to needs."[330] No pope has ever said anything like that about socialism.

If the grand teachers of the Catholic Church saw the inherent problems of socialism, why are so many secular intellectuals drawn to it?

Capitalism has a role for the state, but it is minimal compared to the oversized role that socialism requires. Intellectuals who are convinced of the wonders of social engineering prefer the socialist model because it allows them, or their surrogates, to take command of the state and

[328] Ibid., 17.
[329] Ibid., 20–21.
[330] Charles E. Rice, *50 Questions on the Natural Law* (San Francisco: Ignatius Press, 1993), 288.

reorder society. Socialism gives them power. This power extends far beyond changing the economy: it extends to changing what it means to be a human being.

Hollander captures the essence of this observation: "Intellectuals critical of their society must believe that social institutions superior to those of their own society can be created."[331] Typically alienated from their own society, they look to find solace in other societies. Militantly secular, they search to find meaning, community, and wholeness in something other than organized religion. They epitomize what Max Weber called a world of "disenchantment," the fruit of which is secularization. Hollander sees the irony in all of this. "It is one of the paradoxes of our times that intellectuals, once the vanguard of secularization," he notes, "seem to have become its struggling victims, unwilling or unable to come to terms with an existence, personal and social, that offers so few authentic versions of 'enchantment.'"[332]

In 1937, Orwell nailed it when he observed that "one sometimes gets the impression that the mere words 'Socialism' and 'Communism' draw towards them with magnetic force every fruit-juice drinker, nudist, sandal-wearer, sex-maniac, Quaker, 'Nature Cure' quack, pacifist and feminist in England."[333] Well said.

It is certainly true that lots of nutty intellectuals are desperately trying to find purpose in the promise of socialism, so deracinated have they become. Hollander sees in

[331] Hollander, *Political Pilgrims*, 8.
[332] Ibid., 29.
[333] Ibid., 417.

them a "spiritual emptiness" that is constantly gnawing at them. The alienation they feel from society is also a function of their mad quest to rule. Louis Feuer, a brilliant social philosopher, said it best: "The frustration of their will to rule has been the deepest unconscious source of the intellectual's alienation."[334] It's always about power.

To understand why intellectuals gravitated to socialism early on, we can do no better than listen to what former socialist intellectuals have had to say about their own journeys. Sidney Hook, the great political philosopher, is a particularly good example.

I studied under Hook when I was an undergraduate at NYU. He had a great effect on me. His honesty was matched only by his logical acumen; he was a splendid source of intellectual inquiry.

Like so many New York intellectuals in the 1930s, Hook became despondent with capitalism, blaming it for the Depression. His eyes turned toward the Soviet Union, which was where the socialist dream was expected to materialize. Tutored by his socialist mentor, John Dewey, he wanted to believe that the Soviet Union would prove to be a model for Western nations. But he later came to regret his stance, and indeed became one of the most persuasive critics of Communism and socialism in the world—whereupon he incurred the wrath of left-wing professors and students who leveled vicious assaults against him.

[334] Ibid., 47.

In his autobiography, Hook explained why he fell for socialism. "I was guilty of judging capitalism by its operations and socialism by its hopes and aspirations; capitalism by its works and socialism by its literature." He added that those who identify with left-wing ideas were making the same mistake.[335]

The same phenomenon is at work today. Left-wing intellectuals judge America by comparing the hopes and aspirations of the American Creed to existing conditions. They do not notice how far we have come; they do not compare our current domestic conditions to other countries around the world. The game they are playing means we will always fail to measure up to expectations. We will always lose—but they will always win, by taking power.

Loving the Masses

Intellectuals have one rule for judging themselves, and another for judging everyone else. In their bifurcated world, their good intentions matter gravely in judging themselves; but for the rest of us mortals, it is what we do that counts. "Do as I say and not as I do" is one of their most defining characteristics.

Intellectuals love the masses; but they don't like actual people. It is easy to love people in the abstract. It's much harder to love imperfect flesh-and-blood human beings.

In the classroom, I often saw liberal professors speak warmly about the working class, always hoping the suffering proletariat would finally rebel against their oppressive

[335] Sidney Hook, *Out of Step: An Unquiet Life in the Twentieth Century* (New York: Harper & Row, 1987), 175.

capitalist rulers. But in practice, they never fraternized with the housekeeping staff, the maintenance crew, the cafeteria employees, or any other members of the working class. If anything, they looked down on them. In fact, people who did hang out with the working class were often regarded as unsophisticated. (We saw the liberal professors as snobs and hypocrites.)

The Catholic way was best expressed by Mother Teresa. She helped soothe the fears and conditions of the dispossessed—and she did it for the love of God, not for any material reward. Her approach could not have been more different than that of socialist-minded intellectuals. They always want to save the world. But rarely, if ever, do they have any skin in the game. Mother Teresa saw right through them. To those who say, "I am only one person, I can't save the world," she replied, "If you can't feed a hundred people, then feed just one." Her convictions were quintessentially Catholic. "Jesus said love one another. He didn't say love the whole world."[336]

What the sainted Albanian nun said is rejected by Marxists. It is the job of the state, they say, not individual volunteers, to tend to the needy. That is why they never feel guilt pangs for not personally involving themselves in the lives of the masses. It is not their job.

It was Mother Teresa's Christian-centered outreach to the destitute, the sick, and the dying that drove the English-born atheist Christopher Hitchens to hate her. I debated

[336] Bill Donohue, *Why Catholicism Matters* (New York: Image, 2012), 128.

him several times, and while he and I were both opposed to state-sanctioned abortion, it was his defense of socialism (notwithstanding how well he did profiting from capitalism) and his vile portrait of Mother Teresa that led us to clash. I did not hesitate to tell him that it was his beloved socialism that created the very poor that Mother Teresa served. It drove him mad. He wanted the state to do the job.

Mother Teresa's words and deeds were not inconsistent. She treated people the way she taught her followers to treat them. "It's easy to love those who live far away. It is not always easy to love those who live right next to us."[337] How true—and how particularly true of two of the biggest "humanitarians" adored by the Left, Rousseau and Marx.

Jean-Jacques Rousseau, the intellectual godfather to Robespierre and the architects of the French Revolution, is to this day hailed by left-wing intellectuals for his staunch commitment to championing the rights of the masses, and for his condemnations of their oppressive condition. Too bad he didn't have the same degree of compassion for his own children as he did for the faceless masses.

British philosopher David Hume was one of Rousseau's biggest fans—until he really got to know him. Then he realized that he was "a monster who saw himself as the only important being in the universe."[338] A more recent student of the French secularist, I. W. Allen, was more descriptive. He described Rousseau as a "masochist,

---

[337] Bill Donohue, *The Catholic Advantage: Why Health, Happiness, and Heaven Await the Faithful* (New York: Image, 2015), 195.
[338] Ibid., 159.

exhibitionist, neurasthenic, hypochondriac, onanist, latent homosexual afflicted by the typical urge for repeated displacements, incapable of normal or parental affection, incipient paranoiac, narcissistic introvert rendered unsocial by his illness, filled with guilt feelings, pathologically timid, a kleptomaniac, infantilist, irritable and miserly."[339] These are not exactly the kinds of characteristics we would expect to find in a humanitarian.

In fact, the great Rousseau had a hard time respecting the humanity of his own children. He fathered five illegitimate children by a scullery maid. He never supported them and made sure they wound up in a foundling institution, thus shielding himself from public rebuke. He never even gave his own children names, or recorded their dates of birth. Yet he had the audacity to write a book, *Émile*, about the proper way to raise children. He financially exploited his mistresses and destroyed most of the friendships he made. But as the great chronicler of intellectuals, Paul Johnson, observed, he had a special fondness for cats and dogs. "Rousseau's warmest affection went to animals."[340]

Marx was very much the same. He was a slob who drank heavily and refused to pay his bills; he was a loafer who begged his mother for an advance on his inheritance. His claim to fame was his compassion for the proletariat, the urban factory worker—yet he never befriended them. Like Rousseau, he fathered a child, named Freddy, with his maid, Helene Demuth, known as Lenchen. Though he wrote

[339] Ibid.
[340] Ibid., 162.

endlessly about the exploitation of the workers, he never gave her a dime, providing only room and board.

Nor did he support their son, Freddy. He even arranged for his colleague, Friedrich Engels, to assume paternity. On his deathbed, Engels told one of Marx's daughters, Elena, that the boy he raised, Freddy Demuth, was fathered by her father. She was so devastated that three years later she committed suicide. Marx's other daughter, Laura, also killed herself.

In other words, the two great crusaders for social justice were morally delinquent men who exploited their own families. Yet legions of social science professors continue to cover up their indefensible behavior. If anything, students are told they should emulate these bums.

Sad to say, contemporary "humanitarians" also often do. One of the great champions of the poor, Mitch Snyder, made the TV rounds in the 1980s, always wearing Castro-like fatigues, imploring Americans to give to the homeless. Like Rousseau and Marx, he refused to support his own family. This remained true even when he came into big money (he got a handsome check from Hollywood after his life was portrayed on the screen). But Mitch "cared" about the poor. He "cared" so much that he even lied to a congressional committee about the real number of homeless persons in the nation—he simply made up a figure—hyping the number so it would make him look good.

Snyder was an activist, not an intellectual, but he took his cues from left-wing enthusiasts of Rousseau and Marx. Like them, his public comments about the needy were grossly inconsistent with his behavior toward his own family.

THE FLAWED IDEA OF PERFECTIBILITY

The source of the anger that left-wing activists and intellectuals have for America can be traced back to the flawed idea of perfectibility that took hold during the Enlightenment. This concept was very much a part of the idea of progress that transformed the West for hundreds of years, beginning in the mid-eighteenth century. Robert Nisbet notes that the secularization of the idea of progress meant "detaching it from its long-held relationship with God, making it a historical process activated and maintained by purely natural causes."[341]

Indeed, the question for Enlightenment thinkers was how to perfect man and society in a world without God. Through reason alone, they believed, it was possible to determine the building blocks of a new society, one that would provide freedom and equality for all. But to do that, reason had to be severed from religion. No longer a gift from God, reason became its own god.

Once that idea took hold, the possibilities were endless. The idea of perfection on earth was taken seriously, even to the point of doing away with death. Condorcet, one of the great Enlightenment thinkers, asked if it is unreasonable "to suppose that a period must one day arrive when death will be nothing more than the effect either of extraordinary accidents, or of the slow and gradual decay of the vital powers;

---

[341] Robert Nisbet, *History of the Idea of Progress* (New York: Basic Books, 1980), 172.

and that duration of the middle space, of the interval between the birth of man and his decay, will itself have no assignable limit?"[342]

Alienated intellectuals who have rejected God find themselves searching for transcendent meaning in a rationalistic set of ideas. It propels them to consider the possibility of creating a utopian society.

From a Christian perspective, this is all nonsense. We cannot save ourselves; only God can save us. Redemption is through God alone. As the great Protestant scholar Reinhold Niebuhr said, there is no possibility of creating a perfectly moral social order; we are imperfect and fallen. There can be improvements, yes; but the idea of perfectibility is an illusion.

It all boils down to Original Sin. If it exists, creating a utopian society on earth is impossible; if it doesn't exist, utopia can be realized.

"Man's first sin was pride," said St. Thomas.[343] He was referring, of course, to Adam and Eve, who put their own judgment before the will of God. But the world of intellectuals is full of Adams and Eves, convinced of the power of their ideas to create a new Eden, and full of contempt for our Judeo-Christian heritage.

Original Sin is not explicitly mentioned in the Bible, though the Catholic Church and many Protestants have long accepted it as doctrine. While belief in Original Sin is not part

[342] John Hallowell, *The Moral Foundation of Democracy* (Chicago: University of Chicago Press, 1954), 90.
[343] Rice, *Natural Law*, 192.

of the Jewish tradition, belief in the Ten Commandments certainly implies it. Why all the "thou shalt nots" if mankind inclines toward sinlessness? God chose to command us not to dishonor our family, or to kill or steal, or to covet our neighbor's spouse and property. He did so for a reason: the temptation to take advantage of others is part of human nature.

Although the Catholic Church formally recognizes the idea that we are a fallen people, it was Niebuhr who provided the most cogent defense of Original Sin. "Sin is natural for man in the sense that it is universal but not in the sense that it is necessary," he said.[344] Its appeal to Christians lies in part in its understanding that evil does not come from God but is the result of the choices we make. What God created is good; but man is capable of committing great evil, which allows the devil to triumph. The Catholic Church teaches that "the devil and the other demons were indeed created by God naturally good, but they became evil by their own doing. As for man, he sinned at the suggestion of the devil."[345]

Pope Benedict XVI, in his encyclical *Caritas in Veritate*, observed that "the Church's wisdom has always pointed to the presence of original sin in social conditions and in the structure of society."[346] To this the intellectuals reply that all of the obvious imperfections in society are not baked into

---

[344] Edward T. Oakes, "Original Sin: A Disputation," *First Things*, November 1998, https://www.firstthings.com/article/1998/11/001-original-sin-a-discussion/.

[345] Robert L. Fastiggi, "Original Sin," in *Encyclopedia of Catholic Social Thought*, vol. 3 supplement, 251.

[346] Ibid.

the human condition, but are the result of bad choices made by the power brokers who rule society.

Of all the utopian ideas, the one that best encapsulates the essence of this ideology is the belief that a "new man" can be created. There is no more fantastic, and deadly, idea than this. It shows just how far the secular vision is from the Judeo-Christian understanding of man and society. It also smacks of the sin of pride: God is told to get out of their way — the great thinkers have arrived and will re-create man in their own image.

This explains why so many intellectuals have been attracted to Communism. Unlike the followers of the Abrahamic faiths, who seek redemption in God, the grand intellectual wizards put their faith in a set of secular notions. They want nothing more than to start de novo, to reshape social structures and the dominant culture to allow for the emergence of a "new man." Besides creating the good society, they seek a sense of brotherhood, a sense of community where they can experience wholeness. As Hollander has chronicled, "It is hard to conceive of utopian schemes which exclude the belief in virtually unlimited human potential."[347] Their rejection of Original Sin could not be more transparent.

St. John Paul II addressed this subject several times, and he understood the serious problems attendant to it. He wrote that "if there is no ultimate truth to guide and direct political activity, then ideas and convictions can easily be manipulated for reasons of power."[348] History has proven

---

[347] Hollander, *Political Pilgrims*, 31.
[348] Donohue, *Why Catholicism Matters*, 177.

him right. The denial of truth, a hallmark of so many intellectuals, permits them to advance their agenda without restraint. It's full speed ahead. Yet when the social engineers finally occupy the seats of power, the body count reveals the diabolical nature of their thinking.

VISIONS OF UTOPIA

To appreciate how flawed America's harshest critics really are, consider the kind of world they would have us live in, if their dreams finally did come true. Normal people would hardly regard their creation as a utopia. The lives of Rousseau and Marx are anything but exemplary. And the utopians who came after them offer a more exotic view, particularly with respect to sexuality.

As Paul Johnson notes, Rousseau was the first to argue that human beings could be reshaped by government. The French philosopher spoke of a "new man" who would usher in what he called "perfectibility."[349] To transform man and society, all we needed were the right people in place. Once we resocialize humans and restructure social and cultural institutions, human nature will change.

What was the basis of his optimism? He believed that there had been a time in history when everyone got along just fine. In fact, he supposed that this communal society "must have been the happiest and the most stable of epochs."[350] He did not tell us much more about this happy society, or when

[349] Donohue, *The Catholic Advantage*, 218.
[350] Ibid., 219.

and where it existed. But that it existed was a natural consequence of his conviction that man is basically good.

So how did he explain that things were so messed up?
He had a ready answer: it was the social institutions of family
and church that comprise civil society that were to blame.
They had distorted man's basic nature and were thus responsible for everything that ails us. The path to the progressive
future lay in creating a society where individuals no longer
put their own interests first, but rather prioritized the best
interests of their fellow men. To do this, everyone had to
adopt what he called the "general will"; this is what the
popular will *ought* to be.

It's a good vision, in some ways similar to the Christian
vision of selflessness. But if the institutions such as the family and the church, which are intermediate between the
individual and the state, are really the problem, how is the
"general will" going to be realized? It will be done by the
state, meaning by the agencies of government: they will
crush the traditional family and the church. Then the "new
man" will emerge, liberated from the constraints of traditional institutions. But this will happen not because of his
free will—which Christianity requires—but because the
boot of the state enforces it.

What if the individual balks and rejects this new notion
of freedom? He's out of luck. Rousseau says that "whoever
refuses to obey the general will shall be compelled to do so by
the whole body." This means, he insisted, that the individual

"will be *forced to be free*."[351] This is one of the greatest lines ever written by the sponsors of totalitarianism. It says it all.

Marx's utopia was more ambitious. He was also more detailed in describing how it would unfold. But like Rousseau, there was no room for dissenters.

As we have seen, he lived a pampered existence, refusing to work or support his family. His own mother said she wished her son "would accumulate some capital instead of just writing about it." He wrote endlessly about matters on which he had no experience. But that didn't stop him from championing "scientific communism," even though there was nothing "scientific" about it. Paul Johnson noted that he "never set foot in a mill, factory, mine or industrial workplace in the whole of his life," and he refused invitations to do so.[352]

Marx looked to the proletariat to carry out the revolution against their capitalist oppressors. Under capitalism, he contended, class divisions between property owners and proletariats would become increasingly problematic, eventually leading to the triumph of the proletariat. But this would only happen once the proletariat developed "class consciousness," meaning once they became aware of their oppressed status; intellectuals, of course, would help them discover their oppression.

Once the urban factory workers took control of the state, they would institute a "dictatorship of the proletariat." This

[351] Nisbet, *Idea of Progress*, 241. My emphasis.
[352] Lawrence W. Reed, "Paul Johnson on Why We Should 'Beware Intellectuals,'" Foundation for Economic Education, October 9, 2018, https://fee.org/articles/paul-johnson-on-why-we-should-beware-intellectuals/.

necessary interim stage, Marx said, was required to eliminate all vestiges of capitalism. Once that was done, the "withering away of the State," he said, would soon occur. History has shown us, of course, that once a dictatorship takes hold, the state does not magically wither away. It intensifies.

Common sense to the contrary, Marx believed that the demise of property rights would cause all conflict to cease. There would be no need for a police force, or any security detail. The kinds of destitution and crime that previously existed would all disappear in this new Garden of Eden.

Marx even described how people would live in this idyllic society. In the Communist society, it would be "possible for me to do one thing today and another tomorrow, to hunt in the morning, fish in the afternoon, rear cattle in the evening, criticize after dinner, just as I have in mind, without ever becoming hunter, fisherman, shepherd, or critic."[353]

As many have noted, this kind of society is not what we would expect to be the fruit of advanced capitalism. It appears more like a pre-industrial society.

In the second half of the twentieth century, Marxism finally began to lose its luster. The mass murders that took place under Stalin and Mao—a direct consequence of the totalitarian vision entertained by Marx—made it increasingly difficult to defend such a failed ideology. Still, left-wing malcontents believed that a different type of society could be ushered forth, one that led, if not to a flawless society, at least to individual emancipation.

[353] Nisbet, *Idea of Progress*, 261.

The serial predator, Michel Foucault, was much more interested in a utopian society that allowed for maximum sexual liberation for the individual than he was in improving the plight of the proletariat. Foucault, according to culture critic Roger Kimball, "was fundamentally a child of the Sixties: precocious, spoiled, self-absorbed, full of jejune political statements, wracked by unfulfillable fantasies of absolute ecstasy." This assessment, though harsh, is accurate. Consider the kind of utopian society he envisioned. In an interview he gave in 1968, he suggested that "the rough outline of a future society is supplied by the recent experiences with drugs, sex, communes, other forms of consciousness and other forms of individuality."[354] This vision of the future is exactly what we would expect from a hedonist. Utopian thought had traveled a long way since Rousseau and Marx.

An American utopian of considerable stature, Charles Reich, shared some of Foucault's preoccupation with individual liberation. But he was more ambitious, and more detailed, in his writings. No one captured the idealism of the 1960s better than this Yale law professor. His 1970 book, *The Greening of America*, was a bestseller, and his celebrity status was widely acknowledged. He was the sage of rebellious youth.

Reich contended that America was in a state of crisis, culturally destroying its own people. It could be saved only by a revolution, but not of the military sort. This would be a revolution that "promises a higher reason, a more human

[354] Roger Kimball, "The Perversions of M. Foucault," *New Criterion*, March 1993, https://newcriterion.com/print/article/4714/.

community, and a new and liberated individual. Its ultimate creation will be a new and enduring wholeness and beauty—a renewed relationship of man to himself, to other men, to society, to nature, and to the land."[355] Sounds like a tall order, but to those who spend their time bashing America, and convincing students of the brilliance of their vision for the future, all things are possible.

America, Reich said, had witnessed three stages of consciousness. Consciousness I represented early American history, a time dominated by farmers and small businessmen, ending with robber barons and corruption. Consciousness II emerged during the industrial era and was centered on corporate greed. Highly materialistic, it left a trail of emptiness and injustice in its wake. Consciousness III came to the rescue in the 1960s. Its foundation, he said, was "liberation." It starts with the individual, allowing him to be "free to build his own philosophy and values, his own life-style, and his own culture from a new beginning."[356]

Reich, like the utopians before him, had a rich imagination. Imagine each individual building his own culture. That would be quite a feat.

Individuals are no more capable of building their own culture than they are of building their own social structures. Individuals are born into cultures, and while cultures can change, it takes collective action to change them. Moreover,

[355] Bill Donohue, *The New Freedom: Individualism and Collectivism in the Social Lives of Americans* (New Brunswick, NJ: Transaction Press, 1990), 48.
[356] Ibid.

all cultures are maintained by a consensus regarding norms and values; they are not defined by the preferences of a lone individual. In short, Reich's formulation is sociologically illiterate. But it sure went a long way toward soothing the souls of unhappy young men and women, to say nothing of intellectual malcontents.

The influence of Foucault and Reich was felt by many young Americans. They put their utopian faith in individual liberation, throwing off the shackles of family and religion. But their steady diet of self-indulgence more typically lead to death, spiritual as well as corporeal, not liberation. They found out the hard way, trying to defeat human nature. It doesn't work that way.

THE END OF UTOPIA

Those on the Left who hate America are more radical today than at any time since the 1960s. They are increasingly violent, and even those who do not engage in violence are reluctant to condemn it.

There is a big difference between the violence of the '60s radicals and the violence committed by today's radicals. There was still a glimmer of hope in the 1960s that the utopian society could really be reached; not so today. In the '60s, the violence that accompanied the civil rights movement was done to accelerate the pace of change, to force equal conditions. The violence, though inexcusable, did have a constructive purpose. Today, those who engage in violence are not pursuing a noble end—they are pursuing anarchy. Instead of moving on, coming to terms with the limits of the human condition, today's secular-driven extremists are more like an angry mob that is not only furious with existing conditions but also furious that they are out of ideas. Intellectually spent, they are content to tear things down. They prefer the rubble to the imperfect status quo.

In this regard, no group epitomizes today's brand of angry extremists more than Antifa.

Many Americans know little about Antifa, but they might recognize the group. Mostly, it is a collection of young white men; they wear black clothes and masks, and they played a major role in the riots of 2020. They destroyed parts of Portland, Oregon, taking over neighborhoods and creating "autonomous zones" that denied a police presence. They also savaged Seattle. Their attacks on the police, police cars, and precincts were relentless. The media, for the most part, played down their violence, portraying them as overzealous crusaders for social justice. In point of fact, they are domestic terrorists.

Antifa has no headquarters or command center. It is a loosely organized group of terrorists bent on destroying the social order. Its politics is a blend of left-wing ideas and anarchism, bordering on nihilism. They do not believe in free speech or assembly; and they abhor the courts. Their hatred for religion—and especially for our Judeo-Christian heritage—cannot be exaggerated. Most of all, they hate America.

Unlike the radicals before them, they have no vision for the future. They know what they don't like—which is everything about America —but they have no prescriptions for change and no vision for the future. In other words, they have given up on the left-wing quest for utopia.

Mark Hemingway has studied Antifa. He concluded that, "unlike leftists, its adherents are not seeking to gain the levers of power to build a utopia."[357] They have given up, but this does not mean that they are throwing in the towel. No, like good anarchists, they are determined to tear down existing institutions. They are like the angry boy who delights in smashing his toys and has no thought of rebuilding them.

Antifa's roots are traced to Germany. In 1932, the year before Hitler came to power, the German Communist Party announced the establishment of an "anti-fascist" group that came to be known as "Antifa." In the United States, it wasn't until the late 1980s that the anarchists became active, mostly in Minneapolis and other Midwestern cities. Like the European Antifa, they had Communist and anarchist roots.

Perversely, as journalist Andy Ngo points out, they receive public funding in a backhanded way: they work with the National Lawyers Guild, which is of Communist origin, to sue municipalities following the riots they cause, providing the courts with pictures of the police trying to restrain them, claiming brutality. This is part and parcel of their "direct action" tactics. To put it differently, they exploit weaknesses in the system they seek to destroy, thereby enriching themselves at the public's

---

[357] Mark Hemingway, "Roots of Antifa: This 'Idea' Has Violent Consequences," RealClearInvestigations, October 30, 2020, https://www.realclearinvestigations.com/articles/2020/10/30/roots_of_antif_this_idea_has_violent_consequences_125818.html/.

expense. They also raise money from extremists who are sympathetic to their cause.[358]

To learn more about Antifa, Ngo went undercover and joined them, adopting their style of clothing. He attended meetings in Portland and heard all the left-wing lies told about America. He saw firsthand what "direct action" means. "For months, [Antifa] protesters had dragged passing motorists from their cars, assaulted businesses, and hospitalized journalists whose reporting was disobliging to them—all without law enforcement taking any significant interest. The businesses that still operated did so as in a city under siege."[359] The domestic terrorists also threw flash bombs at children as young as four months old. "Where is your god now?" asked one of their thugs.[360] When Antifa learned that Ngo was a journalist, he was brutally beaten.

It is easy to understand why those who hate America hate capitalism, the cops, and the courts. But what motivates them to take up the causes of abortion and transgender politics? Their idea of liberation, like so many of the intellectuals who inspired them, has to do with freeing everyone from nature and nature's God. They deny the humanity of the

---

[358] Andy Ngo, "Who Funds Antifa Protesters? We All Do," *New York Post*, March 26, 2023, https://nypost.com/2023/03/26/who-funds-antifa-protests-we-all-do/.

[359] Douglas Murray, *The War on the West* (New York: Broadside Books, 2022), 46.

[360] Bill Donohue, "Media Ignore Antifa Assault on Christians," Catholic League, August 11, 2021, https://www.catholicleague.org/media-ignore-antifa-assault-on-christians/.

unborn child and they deny the God-given and nature-based differences between men and women.

In 2023, the Department of Justice unsealed documents pertaining to Antifa. It was revealed that Antifa was working (and often sharing members) with Jane's Revenge, the pro-abortion terrorist group that was firebombing crisis pregnancy centers and vandalizing Catholic churches. Ngo pinpointed the connection, saying Jane's Revenge was "a terrorist far-left group connected to Antifa."[361] Both groups have anarchist roots.

Social media dubbed trans activists and Antifa militants as "Trantifa."[362] They are a subgroup of Antifa members committed to the LGBT cause. Like the parent group, these activists employ violence to further their cause. Ngo said, "They're going after parents and what they call cis women, cis girls, and by that I mean biological, real women and girls." This "violent movement," he says, "allows for particularly violent and misogynistic men to take out their hatred against women under the guise of trans-activism or trans rights."[363]

Kara Dansky, a feminist critic of transgenderism, is living proof of Ngo's observations. She was protesting in Oakland

[361] Valerie Richardson, "Antifa Link Cast Jane's Revenge Attacks on Pro-Life Centers in a Radical New Light," *Washington Times*, January 31, 2023, https://www.washingtontimes.com/news/2023/jan/31/antifa-link-casts-janes-revenge-attacks-pro-life/.

[362] James Reinl, "The New Face of Extremism Unmasked: The UN and Republicans Are Watching 'TRANTIFA,'" *Daily Mail*, June 11, 2023, https://www.dailymail.co.uk/new/article-11995903/The-new-face-extremism-unmasked-Republicans-watching-trantifa.html/.

[363] Ngo made his comments on *Fox News Tonight*, June 14, 2023.

against the California prison system that allows men who identify as a woman to serve their sentences in women's prisons when Trantifa activists attacked her. She described the masked activists as men who could easily overpower women. "It's inevitable that one or more women who stands up for women's sex-based rights is going to be killed," she said.[364]

Antifa, having no vision for a better society, is content to burn it all down. In 2020, a group of Antifa members marched through Lower Manhattan carrying a banner that read "Death to America."[365] That is their goal, and they are not shy about stating it in public.

Antifa's chosen tactic is one of "insurrectionary anarchism"; they want to destroy America. Even sympathetic liberals, such as *New York Times* editorial writer Farah Stockman, know they are going nowhere. She aptly notes that "they are experts at unraveling an old order but considerably less skilled at building a new one." She even castigates them for pretending they are protesting such things as police brutality when in fact their only goal is "insurrection for insurrection's sake."[366]

So where does this leave the Left? It should be obvious that they are angry at the status quo. Less obvious, however, is that, because they have no vision for the future, they have turned their anger inwards. They are raging against

[364] Reinl, "Extremism Unmasked."
[365] Andy Ngo, *Unmasked: Inside Antifa's Radical Plan to Destroy Democracy* (New York: Center Street, 2021), 20.
[366] Farah Stockman, "The Truth about Today's Anarchists," *New York Times*, September 30, 2020, https://www.nytimes.com/2020/09/30/opinion/anarchists-protest-black-lives-matter.html/.

themselves. When Howard Zinn, once a utopian in the Marxian mode, realized that his vision had failed, he ended up becoming a confessed anarchist.

At the close of the twentieth century, an honest left-wing intellectual, Russell Jacoby, saw what was happening. He declared the belief in utopia to be "stone dead." The fall of the Berlin Wall in 1989 and the collapse of the Soviet Union a few years later were the final nails in the coffin. "A new consensus has emerged: There are no alternatives."[367] Nothing could be more devastating to utopian dreamers than this.

Radicals now have no choice, Jacoby argued, but to put up with a modified liberalism. Stanley Aronowitz, one of the more well-known left-wing writers at the time, said such an outcome was "appalling," but this is what happens, he wrote, when "the left has run out of ideas."[368]

The secular vision that intellectuals harbor is at the heart of their troubles. If they understood the reality of Original Sin, they would be able to appreciate the limitations of the human condition. This, in turn, would temper their utopian ambitions. Over the past few decades, the doom and gloom prognosis as outlined by Jacoby has only gotten worse. The Left may not know how to rebuild society, but it is quite good at tearing it down. What we have today is a blend of anarchism and nihilism.

Niebuhr said it well. "The utopian illusions and sentimental aberrations of modern liberal culture are really all

[367] Russell Jacoby, *The End of Utopia: Politics and Culture in an Age of Apathy* (New York: Basic Books, 1999), xii.
[368] Ibid., 15.

derived from the basic error of negating the fact of original sin. This error ... continually betrays modern men to equate the goodness of men with the virtue of their various schemes for social justice and international peace. When these schemes fail of realization or are realized only after tragic conflicts, modern men either turn from utopianism to disillusionment and despair, or they seek to place the onus of their failure upon some particular social group," never blaming themselves.[369]

History has shown that there was no need for Niebuhr to offer an either-or scenario. It is now abundantly clear that intellectuals are in a state of disillusionment and despair. If only they didn't blame everyone for their sorry condition, they might be able to find the road back.

[369] Oakes, "Original Sin."

Conclusion

THE CULTURAL MELTDOWN THAT we have been witnessing is a direct result of the triumph of a secular vision of morality. The American people are showing signs of resistance to this corrupt moral order, but they will need the help of elites in every major institution in society if normalcy is to be restored.

Over two decades ago, Princeton University bioethicist Peter Singer, a man no one would identify as a conservative, argued that the Left should no longer "deny the existence of human nature, nor insist that human nature is inherently good, nor that it is infinitely malleable."[370] This has always been the position of the Catholic Church, as reflected in her description of Original Sin. But for someone like Singer to acknowledge this truth — if not its

---

[370] Ken Brociner, "Utopianism, Human Nature, and the Left," *Dissent*, Winter 2001, https://www.dissentmagazine.org/article/utopianism-human-nature-and-the-left/.

theological foundation — is highly significant. We have a long way to go, however, before a religious vision of morality is restored.

As we have seen, the religious and secular visions of man and society are profoundly different. One reveres truth; the other denies it. One reverences God-governed liberty; the other worships libertinism. One hopes for equality of opportunity; the other pursues the chimera of equality of outcome. One believes in human nature; the other believes in utopia.

Can there be compromises? For the most part, no, there cannot be. Nor is there some magical "third way." Prudence dictates, however, against an all-or-nothing strategy of Judeo-Christian moral restoration. To successfully move the needle, we need to tailor our approach to what is possible, not to what is ideal. For instance, if the citizens of a given state are not prepared to adopt strict restrictions on abortion, but are open to some restrictions, then the latter objective should be pursued. The goal should be to win, to defeat the secular agenda — and winning means dealing realistically with current circumstances.

If we are to see a restoration of the religious vision of man and society, the Catholic Church will have to become more prominent and start leading again. Too many priests and bishops have allowed the clergy sexual abuse scandal — an abomination that took place mostly between 1965 and 1985 — to lower their profile, especially on moral issues. This is a mistake. The scandal is long over, notwithstanding media efforts to keep it current. (What makes this so exasperating is the fact that the scandal was generated in large part by clerics who adopted the very secular vision of morality, especially with regards to the homosexuality that the media supports.)

We cannot play into the hands of the enemies of the Catholic Church: They want to intimidate the Church and silence her moral voice. We cannot let them.

The hierarchy needs to pay more attention to what lay Catholics want. In 2022, the Catholic League commissioned McLaughlin & Associates to do a survey of Catholics on a range of issues.[371]

When asked how important the Catholic Faith is in their life, nine in ten said it was important. One of the most significant findings was the large number of Catholics who rarely or never attend church but who nevertheless said that their Catholic Faith was important to them: 78 percent said it was. We should never give up on these folks.

Is the Catholic Church an important voice of morality in America? You bet she is: 75 percent agreed. This includes seven in ten of those who rarely or never go to church anymore.

When respondents were asked if the Catholic Church should speak out more on moral issues, the results were encouraging: by a margin of 74 percent to 19 percent, respondents answered affirmatively. This is good news for those members of the clergy who have been reluctant to speak out more forcefully. The laity wants them to be more vocal.

[371] Bill Donohue, "Survey of Catholics Is Mostly Promising," Catholic League, September 19, 2022, https://www.catholicleague.org/survey-of-catholics-is-mostly-promising/.

But the laity also has to speak out more. The days are long over when Fr. Murphy could be expected to do the job alone. This means that lay Catholic activists can no longer settle for addressing the easy issues as a quick way to raise funds. They need to step up when the going gets tough. Holding conferences can be useful; but it can also result in passivity in the face of an anti-Catholic onslaught.

A number of years ago I gave an address before a large audience of New York City policemen. Senator Chuck Schumer was in attendance, and we had a short discussion. I told him that the Catholic League was "theologically Catholic but we are behaviorally Jewish." He was taken aback at first but then smiled approvingly. Catholics have much to learn from Jews. We should never be a doormat for bigots to trample on.

Unfortunately, too many Catholics seem to think that the constant array of Catholic bashing is justified, as if we've somehow earned it. These Catholics have adopted the mindset of our enemies. As explained by theologian Thomas D. Williams, even in the eighteenth century Voltaire maintained that the Christian persecution that took place during the Roman Empire was proper. "It was not the Romans who were intolerant, he contended; rather, it was the Christians who were themselves intolerant by insisting on the uniqueness of their religion and their right to be different."[372] This

---

[372] Thomas D. Williams, *The Coming Christian Persecution: Why Things Are Getting Worse and What You Can Do about It* (Manchester, NH: Crisis, 2023), 112.

position was also shared by Edward Gibbon in his famous chronicles of the Roman Empire.[373]

But Catholic teachings are not the problem. They are the solution. They are not outdated, or in need of revision, as too many Catholics—clergy, religious, and lay—have mistakenly concluded. They are eternal truths about human beings, and about God.

It is not the Catholic Church in Germany that is thriving, after all. It is the Church in Africa where Catholics are faithful to the traditional teachings of the Catholic Church. The Germans want desperately to be relevant, to go with the secular flow, especially on sexual matters. Their churches are collapsing.

Orthodoxy sells, even to young people; heterodoxy does not. Why would anyone want to belong to a church that promotes a moral vision that is indistinguishable from that which is found among the chattering class in the media, or in social media musings? Believers want to belong to something special, not something mundane. Mostly, they want to belong to something true.

Protestant theologian Wolfhart Pannenberg noted that secularism's greatest success "is in the widespread demoralization in the ranks of clergy and theologians who are supposed to proclaim and interpret the truth of the gospel but delude themselves that they are achieving that purpose by adapting Christian faith and life to the

[373] Ibid., 116.

demands of secularism."[374] He counsels that just the opposite is necessary.

Catholics agree. In the Catholic League survey, we found that 66 percent of Catholics said that whether they agreed with most positions in the Catholic Church, or differed on some issues, the Church *should not* change her principles because of public opinion; only 27 percent said the Church should modernize. Even 55 percent of those who rarely or never go to church say the Church should not bend to what is popular.

After asking that question, I followed it up with another: "If the Catholic Church did *not* change her position as many have suggested, how would that affect your commitment to the Church?"

Those who said they would be "more committed" totaled 29 percent; 41 percent said they would be "as committed"—which means that 70 percent of Catholics would be either more committed or just as committed to the Church if she *did not* make the changes that many said she should make. Only 7 percent said they would be less committed.[375]

These findings are encouraging. Contrary to conventional wisdom, Catholics do not want a trendy church. They want one that is true to her roots.

It's true, most Catholics are open to certain changes in Church teachings, for example, with respect to female clergy.

[374] Wolfhart Pannenberg, "Christianity and the West," *First Things*, December 1994, https://www.firstthings.com/article/1994/12/christianity-and-the-west/.
[375] Donohue, "Survey of Catholics."

But there is a big difference between a preference and a demand. Very few Catholics get worked up over these issues the way the media do. If they rejected the Church's teachings on moral issues, they would have left to join a "progressive" church long ago—but they better do it quickly, because "progressive" churches are a dying breed.

The Catholic Church—along with evangelical Christians, Orthodox Jews, Mormons, and Muslims—must hold the line and not bow to secular opinion. Secularism is the heart of our moral crisis; it is responsible for our cultural meltdown. We need to proclaim and defend eternal truths about man and society and the moral imperatives that make for the best of all possible worlds on earth. We don't need to re-create anything. We need to repair to our religious moorings.

Acknowledgments

No author is without the benefit of those who have come before him, especially those who have impacted his life intellectually. The great French student of America, Alexis de Tocqueville, and the equally profound French thinker Emile Durkheim have had a great effect on me. I also owe much to Edmund Burke, the father of conservatism, and to Robert Nisbet and Sidney Hook, two brilliant American scholars.

Charlie McKinney, president of Sophia Institute Press, has assembled a first-class group of editors and marketing strategists. I am grateful to all of them.

I have also benefited from the insights of Catholic League staff members, especially Bernadette Brady-Egan, Mike McDonald, Don Lauer, and Nick Palczewski. Walt Knysz Jr., to whom this book is dedicated, has served as chairman of the board with distinction; his steady support is greatly appreciated.

My family—Valerie, Caryn, Cait, Paul, and Jay, as well as my grandchildren, Grant and Nina—are a tremendous source of joy and happiness. The same is true of my friends and relatives, beginning with Maggie and Mike Mansfield, Linda and Tom Boyle, and the McGetricks (especially Riley). And then there are the most persistently parched people God ever put on this earth—the guys and gals at Doc's. Cheers to all.

INDEX

A

abortion: free speech and, 26; laws, 34; as moral issue, 37; religious-secular divide and, 31, 35–36; restrictions on, 35; satanism and, 84–85; statistics on, 34; strategic approaches against, 258

ACLU (American Civil Liberties Union), 25–26, 103, 129

Adorno, Theodor, 101

adultery, 66

Aesop, 181

affirmative action, 208

Africa, Catholic Church in, 261

Ahmadinejad, Mahmoud, 56–57

Alcorn, Leelah, 155

Alito, Samuel, 24, 75–76

Allen, I. W., 235

Allen, Travis, 174

Altizer, Thomas, 81–82

American Creed, 188–91, 233

anarchy: Butler and, 106; contemporary radicals and, 248–53; individual moral codes and, 33

Anderson, Erica, 148

anomie, 99

anti-Catholicism: Douglass and, 205–8; FBI investigations of, 19–21; secularism and, 82–83; of WASP elites, 15

Antifa, 158, 249–53

Arendt, Hannah, 39–40

Aristotle, 9, 39, 79

assisted suicide, 31. See also suicide

atheists: on abortion, 36–37; Boot as, 89–90; Dawkins as, 142, 197; on death penalty, 36; Democratic party and, 28; Hitchens as, 234–35; Öberg as former, 40–41; Zinn as, 191

Augustine of Hippo, Saint, 90

B

B4U-ACT, 117

Bailey, Michael, 154

Banghart, Blaine, 122–23

Beauvoir, Simone de, 137–38

Becerra, Xavier, 177

Beck, Chris, 148

Beckeld, Benedict, 224

Benedict XVI, Pope, 61–62, 70, 194, 240

Bentham, Jeremy, 32–33

Berlin, Isaiah, 59

Biden, Joseph, 144, 158, 176–77

Big Bang Theory, 41

Black Lives Matter, 104

Blanchard, Ray, 154

Boghossian, Peter, 131

Boies, David, 73–75

Boot, Max, 89–90

Boston Children's Hospital, 167–68

Bowers, Marci, 165

Bowers v. Hardwick, 71

Brown, Jonathan, 196–97

Brown v. Board of Education, 186, 189

Buckley, William F., Jr., 103

Burke, Edmund, 92

Butler, Judith, 106, 122, 138

Buttigieg, Pete, 67–68

C

Calhoun, Laurie, 53

Camp Constitution, 18

capitalism, 138, 189, 192, 221, 228–33, 235, 244–45, 251

Caritas in Veritate (encyclical) (Benedict XVI), 240

Catechism of the Catholic Church, 186

Catholic Church: bashing of, 10, 197, 205–8, 260; on common good, 183; cultural Marxist attacks on, 101–2; Engels and, 10; Enlightenment persecution of, 10; equality, 209; in Germany, 261; on human nature, 257–58; Kinsey's hatred of, 108; Marx and, 10, 228–29; moral voice of, 258–59; on Original Sin, 239–40, 257; postmodern intellectuals and, 54; on racism, 185–86; against secularism, 9; on slavery, 185; on socialism, 228–31; teachings of, 261–63; violence against, 252; Voltaire's hatred of, 10

Catholic League, 23–24, 33, 164, 170, 173, 222, 259, 260, 262

Catholics: discrimination against, 222; political parties and, 27–28

children, targeting of, 116–24

Chomsky, Noam, 113–14

Christian Legal Society, 30

Christian privilege, 214, 215

Christianity: categorical distinctions

in, 6; disdain for, 10–11, 196–97; government attacks on, 16; Roman Empire and, 89–90

Christians: Democratic party's attacks on, 28–29; evangelical Christians, 15; government attacks on, 17–19; increasing intolerance toward, 23–24; intolerance of, 260–61; persecution of, 260; Protestant sects, 15; society and, 41

Cicero, 9, 39

The City of God (Augustine), 90

civil rights movement, 186–88, 193–94, 207–8, 207–12, 248

Clark, Richard M., 130

clergy: demoralization in, 261–62; female clergy, 262–63; sexual abuse scandal, 258–59

Coatsworth, John, 56

Cole, Chloe, 142–44

Collins, William J., 217

Columbus, Christopher, 198–99, 200

common good, 41, 42, 65, 181–83, 230

Communism, 63, 100, 102, 231, 232, 241, 244, 250

Condorcet, 238–39

conscience, evil and, 39–40

consent, as basis of morality, 43–48

conservatives: on family, 32, 103; fear of expressing thoughts, 23; happiness in life, 55–56; on moral issues, 31; racism and, 219; religious students as, 26

constants, secular conception of, 7

Cordileone, Salvatore, 16

COVID-19 pandemic: ethical questions during, 32; medical

Hegel, Georg Wilhelm Friedrich, 3, 263

Hemingway, Mark, 250

Hendershott, Anne, 106–7

heterodoxy, 261

Hirschfeld, Magnus, 95

Hitchens, Christopher, 234–35

Hochstadt, Steve, 184

Hollander, Paul, 228, 231, 232, 241

holy and profane, as categorical distinction, 7

homosexuality: Christian view on, 91, 126; clergy sexual abuse scandal and, 258–59; legalization of, 71–72; in Roman Empire, 90–91; in Weimar Republic, 94–95; as wrong, 66, 67

Hook, Sidney, 232, 233

human condition: limitations, 6, 11; secular vision of, 6

human nature: belief in, 258; Catholic Church on, 9, 69; left-wing intellectuals on, 8, 257–58; religious vision of, 5, 41–42; secular vision of, 6; Ten Commandments and, 77–80

human perfectibility: rejection of idea of, 6; secular vision of, 6

Hume, David, 59–60, 235

Huntington, Samuel, 188

I

id, 11

incest, 43–44, 66, 72, 105, 106

indecent exposure law, 47–48, 49

indigenous peoples, 198–204

individual autonomy: civil liberties and, 42–43; exaltation of, 69–70, 73–74; idolizing of, 45; Mill and Stephen on, 46; secular vision of morality and, 89; as valued over religious norms, 32

intellectuals, culture shaped by, 7–8

intolerance, of moral relativists, 62–63

Islam, 196–97

J

Jackson, Ketanji Brown, 177

Jacoby, Russell, 254

Jaffa, Harry, 66–67, 126

Jane's Revenge, 252

Jensen, Robert, 200–201

Jewish people: Marx on, 221; Nazism, 98; Nazism and, 37–38, 57, 99; redemption in God, 241; society and, 41, 263

John Paul II, Pope Saint, 53–55, 65–66, 80, 230, 241–42

John XXIII, Pope Saint, 65, 186

Johnson, Lyndon, 207–8

Johnson, Paul, 59, 236, 242, 244

Jones, Sarah, 173

Jordan, Jim, 19–21

Joshi, Khyati, 214

Judeo-Christian heritage, 260; moral code of, 4, 5; pleasure principle and, 60; reinvigoration and restoration of, 12, 258; secular vision of morality and, 9; the Torah, 6

Justinian, 91

K

Kemp, Brian, 222

Kendi, Ibram X., 210

Kengor, Paul, 221

About the Author

BILL DONOHUE IS PRESIDENT and CEO of the Catholic League for Religious and Civil Rights. He holds a Ph.D. in sociology from New York University and served for twenty years on the board of directors of the National Association of Scholars. The author of ten previous books, he has appeared on thousands of TV and radio shows.

Sophia Institute

SOPHIA INSTITUTE IS A nonprofit institution that seeks to nurture the spiritual, moral, and cultural life of souls and to spread the gospel of Christ in conformity with the authentic teachings of the Roman Catholic Church.

Sophia Institute Press fulfills this mission by offering translations, reprints, and new publications that afford readers a rich source of the enduring wisdom of mankind.

Sophia Institute also operates the popular online resource CatholicExchange.com. *Catholic Exchange* provides world news from a Catholic perspective as well as daily devotionals and articles that will help readers to grow in holiness and live a life consistent with the teachings of the Church.

In 2013, Sophia Institute launched Sophia Institute for Teachers to renew and rebuild Catholic culture through service to Catholic education. With the goal of nurturing the spiritual, moral, and cultural life of souls, and an abiding respect for the role and work of teachers, we strive to provide materials and programs that are at once enlightening to the mind and ennobling to the heart; faithful and complete, as well as useful and practical.

Sophia Institute gratefully recognizes the Solidarity Association for preserving and encouraging the growth of our apostolate over the course of many years. Without their generous and timely support, this book would not be in your hands.

www.SophiaInstitute.com
www.CatholicExchange.com
www.SophiaInstituteforTeachers.org